LUCY SUMMERS runs her own successful landscape design partnership, the Open Garden Company, which has both national and international clients. As an RHS-qualified horticulturalist she has staged show gardens at the Chelsea Flower Show and has been awarded much-coveted Gold and Silver medals for her garden designs. She also contributes regularly to gardening publications, gives lectures to gardening clubs and organisations, and co-hosted *Britain's Best Back Gardens* for ITV among other television work. She lives in Surrey.

> Trying to find a gardening book that is relevant to your needs isn't as straight-forward as it seems. Whether you are new to gardening or a dab hand, sometimes plant descriptions, including care, maintenance and general gardening jargon, can seem overly complicated or, worse still, just too vague. Greenfingers Guides cut through all this, delivering honest, practical information on a wide variety of beautiful plants with easy-to-follow layouts, all designed to enable you to get the best from your garden. Happy gardening!

GREENFINGERS GUIDES

BORDER FLOWERS

LUCY SUMMERS

headline

Copyright © Hort Couture 2010
Photographs © Garden World Images Ltd
except those listed on p. 128

The right of Lucy Summers to be identified as the Author
of the Work has been asserted by her in accordance with
the Copyright, Designs and Patents Act 1988.

First published in 2010
by HEADLINE PUBLISHING GROUP

1

Lucy Summers would be happy to hear from readers
with their comments on the book at the following
e-mail address: lucy@greenfingersguides.co.uk

The Greenfingers Guides series concept was originated
by Lucy Summers and Darley Anderson

A CIP catalogue record for this title is available from
the British Library

ISBN 978 0 7553 1760 8

Design by Isobel Gillan
Printed and bound in Italy by Canale & C.S.p.A.

Headline's policy is to use papers that are natural,
renewable and recyclable products and made from wood
grown in sustainable forests. The logging and
manufacturing processes are expected to conform to the
environmental regulations of the country of origin.

HEADLINE PUBLISHING GROUP
An Hachette UK Company
338 Euston Road
London NW1 3BH

www.headline.co.uk
www.hachette.co.uk
www.greenfingersguides.co.uk
www.theopengardencompany.co.uk

ACKNOWLEDGEMENTS
My thanks to Darling, Zoe, Serena, Lorraine, Josh,
Charlotte and Isobel. And especially to Mark and Elle.

OTHER TITLES IN THE GREENFINGERS GUIDES SERIES:

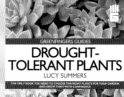

Climbers and Wall Shrubs
ISBN 978 0 7553 1758 5

Drought-Tolerant Plants
ISBN 978 0 7553 1759 2

Fruit and Vegetables
ISBN 978 0 7553 1761 5

Contents

Introduction 6

Choosing border flowers 8
   Using this book 9

Spring 10

Summer 36

Autumn 83

Winter 98

Planting with perennials 101
   Designing a flower border 101
Aspect 105
   Sun and shade 105
   Shelter 105
Soil 106
   Types of soil 106
   Improving the soil 107

Growing 109
   Buying 109
   Planting 109
   Mulching 111
   Watering 111
   Weeding 112
   Deadheading 112
   Cutting back 113
Hardiness 114
Problems 114
   Leaf and stem pests 114
   Plant diseases 116
Propagation 119
   Dividing perennials 119
   Growing perennials from seed 119
   Growing perennials from cuttings 121
The gardening year 122

Border perennials for
 specific purposes 124
Plant index 127
Picture credits 128

Introduction

As a child I stood gawping at my first sighting of an Oriental poppy – a crimson extravaganza, the size of a dinner plate with a sooty black middle. It was an absolute wonder to me that a plant could be so spectacular. Obviously I didn't stay and wonder too long (I had a busy playground itinerary of hide and seek and daisy chains ahead) but the memory is still vivid: poppies make me as happy today as a stray goat on an unattended allotment! Although I have studied plants extensively since then, I can say with absolute conviction that flowers appeal to the senses in a way no textbook ever could. No botanical description can ever do justice to the sumptuous, frilled edges of deeply pleated peonies or impart the full sweetness of phlox, caught on a summer's evening.

I started by 'helping' in my uncle's garden, which was a modest suburban affair, divided equally between a veggie-growing patch and an area completely filled with shrub roses and dahlias. The smell of freshly podded peas intermingled with the spicy fragrance of old roses makes for an intoxicating bouquet even now. That odd aroma transports me back to being knee-high, socks falling round my ankles, my face hot, sticky, and dusty with dirt smudges and my little head filled with no more innocent agenda than sunbeams and the unfailing treat of tinned fruit salad with evaporated milk for tea. Carefree days.

Flowers are definitely an emotional thing. Today, I just can't resist the rough and tumble of a cottage garden, a jumble of flower colour and those old traditional favourites: astrantias, foxgloves, delphiniums, scabious and verbascums.

And where we bring flowers to a garden, we automatically bring wildlife. Plant up a few flowering perennials on a bare patio and suddenly butterflies, hoverflies and the placid bumble bee will find their way to your patch. The wildlife factor cannot be overlooked: their sounds in a garden, from the joyful crescendo of the birds' morning chorus to the gentle droning of pollinating insects and the light-as-a-feather whirling of butterflies, contrive to create a rare, heady cocktail of blissful fascination.

There are so many fabulous plants out there, just waiting for you and me to discover them; we'll never get to grow them all before we die, no matter how hard we try. That is the wonder of flowering plants: so many flowers, so little time. Each of them has their own rich diversity of colour, exotic or simple, often fragrant blooms and their funny little habits and preferences, but all have the potential to bring unbelievable cheer and loveliness to simple gardeners like us.

Choosing border flowers

Planning what to grow in a border is a blissful occupation. The range and variety of flowering border plants is simply enormous. The full spectrum of the rainbow is represented, with wonderful flower variations and spectacular leaf shapes on offer to the adventurous gardener. There are bold reds and oranges to suit the exhibitionist; soft muted pastels for the gentler temperament and many of these combine with heavenly fragrance, turning the garden into a floral paradise.

Planting with border perennials is not just fun but incredibly artistic and creative. Some years you hit it just right. Other years, for some reason, the combinations don't look as appealing. Perhaps the spread of one plant increased too much or too little, or excessive wet weather prevented the border reaching its best. On the other hand, plants that self-seed can sometimes place themselves in absolutely the right spot, teaming up with complementary neighbouring plants through no effort of yours. In which case, shamelessly take the credit from Mother Nature for thinking of such a marvellous combination!

The majority of the plants included in this book are hardy herbaceous perennials. I have chosen to focus on flowering perennials because they are lovely – and, for once, they are a pleasure we can indulge in which isn't injurious to health! Perennials take very little effort to look after and are just so exciting for the colour, flower shape and fragrance they bring to our garden beds and borders. Plant in plenty and reject frugality in your flower borders.

Most perennials flower in summer. Some come into flower earlier, in spring, or continue to flower into autumn, but very few indeed flower in winter. So if you are only growing hardy herbaceous perennials (like most of the plants in this book), don't expect to see much going on in the winter months. However, flowering perennials can be grown with evergreen foliage plants, ornamental grasses, shrubs and trees in the flower border: by planting a mixture of all these, there will still be plenty to admire come winter.

Our plant choices are influenced by so many different stimuli. However, I would hazard a guess that the most powerful associations come from fond childhood memories or an unexpected draught of a long-forgotten fragrance.

And we are bombarded on a daily basis by new plants arriving on the gardening scene: in glossy gardening magazines and sophisticated coffee-table books; at national flower shows, visits to 'open' gardens or Sunday outings to stately homes; or even something enticing in a friend's garden.

We may be better informed than ever before about plants, but they appeal to each of us uniquely. Who cares whether these wondrous perennials are in or out of vogue? Does it matter that it doesn't have an AGM? Give it a try. Perhaps the colour is a trifle brash for the common herd? Bah! Combining golden tickseed, smouldering purple heucheras and tall, fiery orange or red montbretias may not be everybody's cup of tea, but I love them together. Herbaceous perennials are there to please the eye and appease your spirit. If it makes you happy, plant it.

Almost without exception, the border plants included here are easy to grow and maintain. Most are weather hardy and don't need much in the way of special conditions, but all will make your garden a more interesting, luxuriant place. The real difficulty has been deciding which to leave in and which to leave out. Unfortunately, evergreen perennials that don't flower, including many beautiful grasses and ferns, have been given a miss so we can really concentrate on border perennials. Shrubs have also been excluded, for the same reason. But I have included a few plants with exceptional foliage.

Like a child in a sweetshop with eyes far too big for the floral assortment on offer, I have sought to offer you some of the finest border plants around (and for most plants I've suggested alternative varieties or species, in different colours and heights, for you to play with). Many beautiful plants had to be left out because of space limitations, but here is a selection of some really choice perennials that will combine to make your garden a beautiful, diverse space.

Echinaceas will attract bees into the wildflower garden

Using this book

Each plant listed is categorised according to season and its eventual height, with useful, practical cultivation advice that will encourage you to grow with ever greater enjoyment, creativity and confidence. More detailed information, covering all the different elements mentioned in the profiles, and including help with planting and propagation, will be found after the plant profiles. Lists of plants for specific purposes can be found at the back of the book.

Throughout the book, plants are arranged seasonally, but in practice the corresponding months will vary according to local weather patterns, regional differences and the effects of climate change. Additionally, the flowering times of many plants span more than one season. The seasons given are based in the British Isles, and should be thought of as a flexible guide.

Early spring	March	Early autumn	September
Mid-spring	April	Mid-autumn	October
Late spring	May	Late autumn	November
Early summer	June	Early winter	December
Mid-summer	July	Mid-winter	January
Late summer	August	Late winter	February

Latin names have been given for all the plants in this book because these are the names that are universally used when describing plants; the Latin name should be recognised by the garden centre, and with any luck you will be sold the right plant. Common names have also been given, but these vary from country to country, and even within a country, and a plant may not be recognised by its common name.

Skill level is indicated by one of three ratings: **EASY, MEDIUM** or **TRICKY**

Many of the plants chosen for this book have been given the Award of Garden Merit (AGM) by the Royal Horticultural Society (RHS). This is a really useful pointer in helping you decide which plants to buy. The AGM is intended to be of practical value to the ordinary gardener, and plants that merit the award are the cream of the crop. The RHS is continually assessing new plant cultivars and you can be sure that any plant with an AGM will have excellent decorative features and be:

- easily available to the buying public
- easy to grow and care for
- not particularly susceptible to pests or diseases
- robust and healthy

SPRING

Everyone loves a summer garden, but for me, spring has the edge as the most marvellous time in the gardening year. Every green in nature's palette is on show, providing a perfect foil for the flowers, fruits and berries to come. Dark, iron earth warms and awakes, as bulbs peep timidly from their underground lairs, leaf buds fatten and unfurl, clothing the shivering limbs of winter trees, and thin shafts of lemony sun lure us from our winter inertia. Although spring plants rarely achieve the great heights of summer-flowering garden perennials, there are some wonderful plants out there that can help you create the perfect spring border.

Ajuga reptans 'Catlin's Giant'
Bugle

⬆ 25cm/10in ⬌ 90cm/3ft   EASY

This rhizomatous perennial from Europe and Asia has a carpeting habit, with slightly quilted evergreen leaves and short, whorled spires of deep blue flowers in spring. 'Catlin's Giant' has slightly larger leaves than the more common *A. reptans*, flushed a sumptuous deep claret to black. Ajuga is prone to mildew, so spray with skimmed milk diluted with water at the first sign of trouble. *A.r.* 'Burgundy Glow' has purple-pink leaves; *A.r.* Black Scallop has scallop-edged leaves in burgundy black.

> **BEST USES** Very effective ground cover for slopes or in lightly shaded woodland areas; delightful at the front of the border or edging paths

FLOWERS April to May
SCENTED No
ASPECT North, east or west facing, in a sheltered position; full sun to partial shade
SOIL Any fertile, humus-rich, well-drained soil; add organic matter before planting
HARDINESS Fully hardy at temperatures down to -15°C/5°F; needs no winter protection
DROUGHT TOLERANCE Good, once established
PROBLEMS Aphids; powdery mildew; foliage may fade or scorch in bright sunlight
CARE Cut back stems after flowering for a second flush; use a mower (with the blades high) on a large patch
PROPAGATION Division in autumn or spring; sow seed at 10°C/50°F in spring; detach rooted plantlets and pot up in spring or early autumn

Allium schubertii

⬆ 30–60cm/12–24in ⬌ 20cm/8in   EASY

Alliums are hardy bulbous perennials from dry, rocky hillsides from Asia to eastern Europe that offer architectural impact. This eye-catching species has aromatic, strappy, fresh green leaves which start to die back as the plant comes into flower, but it is the large, spherical flower globes (30cm/12in), the size of a football, comprising myriad tiny, star-shaped pinky-purple flowers, borne on smooth, straight, slender stems, some short, some taller, that set this apart as a plant with star quality. Once the flowers fade, the flower heads take on an attractive skeletal form.

BEST USES Marvellous as vertical or sculptural accents in the traditional or contemporary border; bees and butterflies adore this plant

FLOWERS May to June
SCENTED Onion-scented leaves, when crushed
ASPECT South, east or west facing, in a sheltered or exposed position; full sun
SOIL Any fertile, well-drained soil
HARDINESS Frost hardy at temperatures down to -5°C/23°F; needs winter protection in colder areas
DROUGHT TOLERANCE Good, once established
PROBLEMS Onion fly; downy mildew, onion white rot and powdery mildew
CARE Plant bulbs 15cm/6in deep and 40cm/16in apart, in autumn; foliage dies back naturally
PROPAGATION Sow ripe seed in late summer to early autumn; division in late summer or autumn; pot up bulblets in autumn

Anemone sylvestris
Snowdrop anemone

⬆ 40cm/16in ⬌ 40cm/16in   EASY

An easy-to-grow, European herbaceous perennial with a suckering habit that makes neat, dense mounds of deeply lobed, mid-green leaves from which arise green, wiry stems with small, nodding, scented flower buds that suddenly lift upwards, faces to the sun, to reveal simple, shallow, pure white, fluttering, papery flowers with golden centres, up to 8cm/3in across. It is a darling plant and should be more widely grown.

BEST USES Ideal for edging north-facing borders and beds where you can appreciate its subtle fragrance as you pass; an ideal plant for coastal gardeners; a mainstay of the cottage garden; great as a cut flower

FLOWERS April to May
SCENTED Yes
ASPECT Any, in a sheltered or exposed position; full sun to partial shade
SOIL Any fertile, moist, well-drained soil
HARDINESS Fully hardy at temperatures down to -15°C/5°F; needs no winter protection
DROUGHT TOLERANCE Poor
PROBLEMS Caterpillars, slugs and snails; powdery mildew
CARE Deadhead spent blooms regularly to encourage further flowering; cut back to just above ground level in late winter or spring
PROPAGATION Division in early spring

Bergenia 'Bressingham White' 🎖
Elephant's ears

⬆ 30–45cm/12–18in ⬌ 45–60cm/18–24in   **EASY**

The main appeal of this evergreen Asian perennial is in its large, leathery, oval, glossy dark green leaves (15–18cm/6–7in long). The simple, pure white flowers, flushed pink when open, with yellow-green centres, droop slightly on attractive sturdy, stubby red stems, and are a bonus from mid to late spring. *B.* 'Abendglut' has double, rosy pink flowers; *B.* 'Bressingham Ruby' has rosy flowers and leaves that redden in winter.

BEST USES Excellent as low-maintenance ground cover on slopes or banks; ideal for coastal gardens

FLOWERS April to May

SCENTED No

ASPECT Any, in a sheltered or exposed position; full sun to full shade

SOIL Any fertile, humus-rich, moist, well-drained soil

HARDINESS Fully hardy at temperatures down to -15°C/5°F; needs no winter protection

DROUGHT TOLERANCE Good, in shade, once established

PROBLEMS Caterpillars, slugs, snails and vine weevil; leaf spot

CARE Remove faded flower spikes and tatty-looking leaves; mulch with organic matter in spring

PROPAGATION Not true from seed; division in spring or autumn every 3–5 years

GREENFINGER TIP *The leaves may darken slightly after harsh winters, but new ones soon grow*

Brunnera macrophylla 'Jack Frost' 🎖
Siberian bugloss

⬆ 40cm/16in ⬌ 60cm/24in   **EASY**

This deciduous clump-forming herbaceous perennial from the Caucasian mountains is one of my all-time favourites: it manages to be tough, dependable and pretty. It has the loveliest, slightly hairy, heart-shaped, silver-white leaves that are heavily veined with fresh green (arguably the best feature of the plant) and cheerful airy sprays of bright blue forget-me-not flowers in spring. It scores 10/10 for spring foliage and flower. *B.m.* 'Dawson's White' has green leaves edged cream and tiny blue flowers.

BEST USES Takes some beating as ground cover; an absolute delight planted alongside spring-flowering bulbs and hardy ferns in the cottage garden or spring flower border; rabbit proof

FLOWERS April to June

SCENTED No

ASPECT Any, in a sheltered position; partial shade

SOIL Any fertile, humus-rich, moisture-retentive soil; good for heavy clay

HARDINESS Fully hardy at temperatures down to -15°C/5°F; needs no winter protection

DROUGHT TOLERANCE Good, but only for short bursts

PROBLEMS None; leaves may scorch in full sun

CARE Cut flower stems back after flowering; cut tatty leaves to just above ground level in autumn or early spring

PROPAGATION Division after flowering; sow seed in spring at 10°C/50°F

Centaurea montana 'Gold Bullion'
Mountain knapweed

⬆ 40cm/16in ⬌ 40cm/16in EASY

Knapweeds are a European family of perennial and annual plants, mainly in blue, pink, yellow and white forms. This clump-forming rhizomatous perennial is outstanding for its lance-shaped golden leaves, which make a change from the more usual green hues of the species, and very pretty, shaggy, deep blue petals radiating out from deep purple centres, with almost black stamens, tipped white. It is an easy, low-maintenance perennial, unfussy about soil as long as it isn't wet and, in my experience, will tolerate light shade. Other varieties include *C.m.* 'Alba' (white flowers), *C.m.* 'Carnea' (pink flowers) and *C.m.* 'Parham' (lavender flowers).

BEST USES Ideal at the front of borders and in the cottage garden; lovely for the wildlife garden as nectar-collecting insects love it

FLOWERS May to July

SCENTED No

ASPECT Any, in a sheltered or exposed position; full sun to partial shade

SOIL Any fertile, well-drained soil

HARDINESS Fully hardy at temperatures down to -15°C/5°F; needs no winter protection

DROUGHT TOLERANCE Good, once established

PROBLEMS Powdery mildew in dry weather

CARE Cut down to ground level after flowering to encourage new growth; mulch annually in spring

PROPAGATION Division in autumn or spring; sow seed in pots in a cold frame in spring

Chaerophyllum hirsutum 'Roseum'
Hairy chervil

⬆ 60cm/24in ⬌ 30cm/12in EASY

Found in meadows and hedgerows across Spain and France, this easy-to-manage, upright, clumping deciduous perennial deserves to be seen more often. It looks a bit like a pink version of cow parsley, with bright green, fringed, ferny, apple-scented leaves that are often flushed with claret hues, and slender, arching, reddish stems topped with massed tiny umbels of soft pink flowers from spring to summer. *C. hirsutum* has white flowers, with serrated, toothed, fresh green leaves.

BEST USES Lovely in the woodland or wildflower garden or a shady border; ideal for attracting pollinating insects

FLOWERS May to June

SCENTED Aromatic leaves

ASPECT Any, in a sheltered or exposed position; full sun to partial shade

SOIL Any fertile, humus-rich, moisture-retentive soil

HARDINESS Fully hardy at temperatures down to -15°C/5°F; needs no winter protection

DROUGHT TOLERANCE Poor

PROBLEMS Aphids, slugs and snails; powdery mildew

CARE Deadhead spent flowers to prevent self-seeding; mulch annually in early spring

PROPAGATION Sow seed in pots in a cold frame in autumn or spring; mature colonies self-seed

Convallaria majalis ♔
Lily of the valley

⬆ 23cm/9in ⬌ 30cm/12in   EASY

Lily of the valley is a rhizomatous perennial, originating in woodlands and meadows in temperate climates. Its crisp, clean lines make a joyous sight in late spring, with smooth, dark green oval leaves and clusters of highly fragrant, pendent, tiny, white belled flowers held on short, smooth stems. *C.m.* var. *rosea* has pink flowers, and there is an unusual variegated form, *C.m.* 'Albostriata', with bright green leaves, striped with very distinct creamy white vertical lines, which is worth hunting down (remove any plain green leaves to preserve the variegation).

> **BEST USES** An elegant addition to a woodland garden; makes effective ground cover, although not quick to colonise; combines very well with spring-flowering bulbs; the fragrance is heavenly

FLOWERS May to June
SCENTED Highly scented flowers
ASPECT Any, in a sheltered position; partial to full shade
SOIL Any fertile, humus-rich, moisture-retentive soil
HARDINESS Fully hardy at temperatures down to -15°C/5°F; needs no winter protection
DROUGHT TOLERANCE Poor
PROBLEMS *Botrytis* (grey mould)
CARE Mulch with organic matter annually in spring
PROPAGATION Division of rhizomes in autumn

GREENFINGER TIP *This can be a struggle to establish: buy pot-grown plants rather than dried crowns, plant in well-prepared soil, then leave alone to settle*

Corydalis 'Kingfisher' ♔

⬆ 15cm/6in ⬌ 10cm/4in   EASY

There are some 300 species of corydalis, commonly available in blue and yellow hues. This hybrid is a tuberous perennial producing mounds of ferny, divided mid-green foliage, with short, smooth stems topped with flower buds that open to spikes of slightly pendent, tubular sky blue flowers, with pronounced lips, rather like snapdragons. It is dormant in winter but flowers pretty much non-stop otherwise, only pausing, it seems, in autumn, which makes this a real value for money plant. It has a more restrained habit than the common *C. lutea* (yellow flowers and invasive) and, as it is sterile, doesn't wander off where it is not wanted. My own personal favourite, though a different species, is the tuberous *C. malkensis* (15cm/6in), with tubular white flowers in spring.

> **BEST USES** Ideal in a spring border or woodland garden; perfect for low planting at the front of borders; also does well in containers

FLOWERS March to September
SCENTED No
ASPECT South, east or west facing, in a sheltered position; full sun to partial shade
SOIL Any fertile, humus-rich, well-drained soil
HARDINESS Fully hardy at temperatures down to -15°C/5°F; needs no winter protection
DROUGHT TOLERANCE Poor
PROBLEMS Slugs and snails
CARE Mulch with organic matter in spring
PROPAGATION Division once dormant

Epimedium grandiflorum ♈

🔼 30cm/12in ↔️ 30cm/12in   **EASY**

Epimediums are valued for their fine foliage (some are evergreen, others deciduous) and dainty spring flowers in colours ranging from coral reds, pinks and whites to yellows. This rhizomatous herbaceous perennial of Asian origin has tapering, heart-shaped fresh green leaves, which are blushed bronze when young, and thin, wiry stems topped with spurred, slightly pendent rose pink, white and violet flowers. Other notable choices are *E.g.* 'Rose Queen' ♈ with rose pink flowers and *E.g.* 'Nanum' ♈ with pure white flowers (both 30cm/12in).

BEST USES A dainty plant for the cottage garden or small raised border; works well in a shady, north-facing bed; useful as edging or small clumps dotted through low planting; makes ideal ground cover

FLOWERS April to May
SCENTED No
ASPECT North, east, or west facing, in a sheltered position; partial shade
SOIL Any fertile, moist, humus-rich, well-drained soil
HARDINESS Fully hardy at temperatures down to -15°C/5°F; needs no winter protection
DROUGHT TOLERANCE Poor
PROBLEMS Vine weevil
CARE Cut back tatty foliage in early autumn or late winter
PROPAGATION Division in autumn or after flowering; sow ripe seed immediately in pots in a cold frame

Erythronium 'Pagoda' ♈
Dog's-tooth violet/Trout lily

🔼 35cm/14in ↔️ 10cm/4in   **MEDIUM**

This robust, tuberous perennial from North America forms small clumps of handsome, pointed, deep green, marbled leaves and bears a dozen or so delicate, reflexed, nodding sulphur yellow flowers that reveal distinctive pale yellow anthers; these are carried on smooth, arched stems held high above the foliage. Sharing similar characteristics, *E. californicum* 'White Beauty' ♈ has white flowers, and *E. revolutum* 'Knightshayes Pink' has pink flowers and self-seeds freely; both are 35cm/14in tall. (Sap can cause skin irritation.)

BEST USES Plant in drifts in woodland or a shady border, where they will colonise rapidly, or at the front of a border, slightly shaded by taller plants

FLOWERS March to April
SCENTED No
ASPECT Any, in a sheltered or exposed position; partial shade
SOIL Any fertile, moist, well-drained, humus-rich soil
HARDINESS Fully hardy at temperatures down to -15°C/5°F; needs no winter protection
DROUGHT TOLERANCE Poor
PROBLEMS Slugs and snails
CARE Plant tubers 15cm/6in deep and apart; keep well watered in dry periods
PROPAGATION Division in autumn; sow ripe seed immediately in autumn

GREENFINGER TIP *Scatter the tubers on the ground and plant where they fall for a natural effect*

EUPHORBIAS
Spurge

Found from the tropics of Africa and Asia to temperate regions across Europe, in woodlands or adorning dry, arid hillsides, euphorbias are grown for their achingly bright limey flowers (which are not true flowers but leaf bracts) and fine foliage.

They range from small annuals and perennials (10cm/4in) to tall, architectural perennials and shrubs (1.2m/4ft), many with sculptural leaves.

They flower from February right through to November, depending on the variety, and enjoy a wide range of soils, from dry, hot sunny sites (and the brighter the sun, the stronger the colour) to heavy clay or humus-rich shade. With more than 2000 to choose from, there is a variety to suit almost any area of the garden. Most are easy to grow and need little maintenance.

I have noticed that rabbits and goats don't eat them, presumably because the stems bleed an undesirable milky sap, which can cause skin irritation in humans, so wear gloves to avoid this.

Additional recommended varieties include *E. myrsinites* ♛ (10cm/4in) with silver grey coiling leaves in spring (full sun and well-drained soil); *E. cyparissias* 'Fens Ruby' (48cm/18in) – *see above* – with lemon yellow flowers in early summer (full sun and well-drained soil); *E. Blackbird* (50cm/20in) with red stems and dark green leaves flushed purple (tolerates partial shade, likes well-drained soil), flowering in early summer; *E. schillingii* ♛ (90cm/3ft) has white-ribbed lance-shaped leaves and golden yellow flowers from summer to autumn.

Euphorbia amygdaloides 'Purpurea'
(formerly *E.a.* 'Rubra')

⬆ 60cm/24in ⬌ 30cm/12in   EASY

This bushy, rhizomatous perennial is very architectural with dark, evergreen leaves, flushed burgundy, and stiffly upright, damson-coloured stems that are topped with acid yellow flowers. *E.a.* var. *robbiae* ♛ has light green flowers. Other euphorbias of similar height include *E. × martini* 'Baby Charm', a compact, tidy variety with dark green leaves, tinged pink, and branching red stems carrying pale green flowers from spring to mid-summer, and *E. rigida* ♛, with sprawling green-grey whorled leaves and acid yellow flowers, pink-tinged as they mature in early summer, and an orange centre.

BEST USES Ideal for stunning shape and colour in a contemporary city garden; looks good in woodland and cottage gardens as well as formal borders

FLOWERS April to June
SCENTED No
ASPECT Any, in a sheltered or exposed position; full sun to partial shade
SOIL Any fertile, well-drained soil
HARDINESS Fully hardy at temperatures down to -15°C/5°F; needs no winter protection
DROUGHT TOLERANCE Good, once established
PROBLEMS *Botrytis* (grey mould)
CARE Cut back faded flower stems in autumn, taking care not to cut into new shoots at the base
PROPAGATION Division in spring

Euphorbia polychroma

⬆ 40cm/16in ⬌ 60cm/24in   EASY

This compact, deciduous perennial, with lance-shaped, fresh green leaves on sturdy upright stems, may not be as showy as some of the larger euphorbia cultivars, but has eye-aching, acid yellow flowers and looks marvellous against the fresh green foliage of spring plants and shrubs. By summer it looks a little scruffy, but this is hidden by other plants' leafy growth. *E.p.* 'Candy' (45cm/18in) has grey-green leaves suffused with purple-pink, and sulphur yellow flowers; *E.p.* 'Lacy' (50cm/20in) has pallid green, cream-edged leaves, with pale, creamy yellow flower heads.

BEST USES Its zingy colour makes it a reliable performer in the border; combines well with hardy geraniums as it flowers a good month earlier; pleasing in containers or with spring bulbs

FLOWERS April to May

SCENTED No

ASPECT Any, in a sheltered or exposed position; full sun to partial shade

SOIL Any fertile, humus-rich, moist, well-drained soil

HARDINESS Fully hardy at temperatures down to -15°C/5°F; needs no winter protection

DROUGHT TOLERANCE Excellent, once established

PROBLEMS Aphids; *Botrytis* (grey mould)

CARE Cut back spent flower stems to new growth after flowering

PROPAGATION Division in early spring

Hacquetia epipactis

⬆ 5–15cm/2–6in ⬌ 15–30cm/6–12in   MEDIUM

This is a very under-rated low-growing rhizomatous perennial from European woodlands. Compact clusters of small, luminous green bracts (up to 5cm/2in across) on short stems form soft scallopy mounds, from late winter to early spring. The bracts resemble pale green petals grouped around the yellow centres and are followed shortly afterwards by rounded, shiny emerald green leaves.

BEST USES Excellent as slow-growing carpeting ground cover under trees, or on awkward slopes and banks; ideal in a rock garden or in woodland

FLOWERS February to March

SCENTED No

ASPECT Any, in a sheltered position; partial shade

SOIL Any humus-rich, moist, free-draining soil; add grit to soil to improve drainage before planting; prefers acid to neutral soil

HARDINESS Fully hardy at temperatures down to -15°C/5°F; needs no winter protection

DROUGHT TOLERANCE Poor

PROBLEMS Slugs and snails on young growth

CARE Low maintenance

PROPAGATION Division in spring

GREENFINGER TIP *This plant resents disturbance, so plant it where it can make a spreading carpet in peace*

Hepatica nobilis 'Cobalt'
Liverleaf

⬆ 8cm/3in ⬌ 15cm/6in   MEDIUM

Hepaticas are small, carpeting, semi-evergreen woodland perennials from Europe, Asia and North America, with delicate stalks arising from small, dark green, pointed leaves. This variety is topped with masses of simple, open saucer-shaped, pale royal blue flowers and creamy-coloured anthers, in late winter to early spring, making them a welcome rarity. *H.n.* white-flowered has pure white flowers and *H.n.* 'Pyrenean Marbles' has green and bronze marbled foliage.

> **BEST USES** Ideal for carpeting awkward slopes or banks; good as edging in the cottage garden or spring border; naturalises well among spring-flowering bulbs, but needs time to settle down

FLOWERS February to March

SCENTED No

ASPECT Any, in a sheltered or exposed position; partial shade

SOIL Any fertile, humus-rich, moist, well-drained soil

HARDINESS Fully hardy at temperatures down to -15°C/5°F; needs no winter protection

DROUGHT TOLERANCE Poor

PROBLEMS Slugs and snails

CARE Water regularly; mulch with leafmould in autumn

PROPAGATION Division after flowering or in late winter (may take a season to recover); sow ripe seed immediately in pots in a cold frame in shade (plants grown from seed can take up to three years to flower)

Hosta 'Big Daddy' (*sieboldiana* hybrid)
Plantain lily

⬆ 60cm/24in ⬌ 90cm/3ft   EASY

This clump-forming herbaceous perennial is one of many hybrids from the USA, which come in a bewildering array of leaf colour, size, shape and form and have pretty, trumpet-shaped flowers in pale lavender to white, some very fragrant, borne on leafless stems in summer. This has handsome, puckered, quilted steely blue leaves (30cm/12in long) in spring, which are lovely jewelled in raindrops after a shower, and off-white bell-like flower spikes, held on smooth, bare stems, in early summer. Slugs and snails have a legendary appetite for hostas, but 'Big Daddy' is said to be more resistant to attack than most. *H. sieboldiana* var. *elegans* ♀ (90cm/3ft × 1.2m/4ft) is famed for its large, deeply quilted steely blue-grey leaves.

> **BEST USES** Ideal as ground cover for the woodland garden; adds sculptural accents to the flower border; does well in containers in shady city or courtyard gardens

FLOWERS June

SCENTED No

ASPECT Any, in a sheltered position; partial shade

SOIL Any fertile, moist, well-drained soil

HARDINESS Fully hardy at temperatures down to -15°C/5°F; needs no winter protection

DROUGHT TOLERANCE Poor

PROBLEMS Slugs and snails (relentless!)

CARE Mulch with organic matter annually in spring

PROPAGATION Division from late summer to early spring

Lathyrus vernus ♉
Sweet pea

⬆ 45cm/18in ⬌ 45cm/18in   **EASY**

Associated with the arrival of summer, sweet peas are usually grown as annual climbing plants, so this herbaceous perennial sweet pea is a welcome treat in spring. Found in Turkey, Russia and across Europe, it makes a real change from the more common spring yellows. The unscented flowers often appear before the paired, pointed mid-green leaves, which form low, bushy clumps. Slender, upright stems display clusters of six pea-like, rose pink-purple flowers that age to greeny blue. *L.v.* 'Alboroseus' ♉ (35cm/14in) has pinky white flowers; *L.v.* 'Rosenelfe' (30cm/12in) has pale pink flowers.

> **BEST USES** Ideal for early colour in the cottage garden or borders; try it in pots in light shade

FLOWERS March to June

SCENTED No

ASPECT South, east or west facing, in a sheltered or exposed position; full sun to partial shade

SOIL Any fertile, humus-rich, well-drained soil

HARDINESS Fully hardy at temperatures down to -15°C/5°F; needs no winter protection

DROUGHT TOLERANCE Good, once established

PROBLEMS Aphids, slugs and snails

CARE None; plant dies back after flowering

PROPAGATION Division in spring; sow pre-soaked seed in pots in a cold frame in spring

GREENFINGER TIP *They resent disturbance, so may take a season to recover after division*

Myosotidium hortensia
Chatham Island forget-me-not

⬆ 60cm/24in ⬌ 60cm/24in   **MEDIUM**

This half-hardy New Zealander is a very lovely evergreen perennial, bearing large clusters of small, bright blue forget-me-not flowers on stout stems, above a mound of large, handsome, pleated, glossy leaves (about 30cm/12in wide) with wavy edges. Though it doesn't flower until late spring, it is worth growing for the foliage alone. It needs a sheltered, cool, damp, shady spot to succeed and, with protection, will come through winter well in milder areas and frost-free city centres; if you can offer these conditions, have a go: it is the most elegant of ground-cover plants.

> **BEST USES** Brightens up a gloomy corner at the foot of a north-facing wall in a shady urban garden; grows happily in coastal gardens

FLOWERS May

SCENTED No

ASPECT North or east facing, in a sheltered position with protection from cold winds; partial shade

SOIL Any fertile, moist, humus-rich, well-drained, acid to neutral soil

HARDINESS Half hardy down to 0°C/32°F; needs winter protection

DROUGHT TOLERANCE Poor

PROBLEMS Slugs and snails

CARE Remove faded flower spikes; mulch annually; provide winter protection

PROPAGATION Division in spring; sow ripe seed in pots in a cold frame in autumn

Narcissus 'Doctor Hugh' ♀
Daffodil

⬆ 45cm/18in ⬌ 10cm/4in   **EASY**

Come spring, daffodils are the first plants that come to mind. They are bulbous perennials, originally from Europe to North Africa, with strappy, erect, narrow, smooth green leaves and leafless stems holding the flowers. There are thirteen categories, with large or small flower trumpets and solitary or multiple flowers, in shades of gold, orange, white and pinky tones. Heights range from 10cm/4in to about 60cm/24in, and they increase each year, making a natural clump within three years. This is one of the 'small-cupped' varieties, each stem bearing a perfectly symmetrical six-petalled flower of the purest white, with a short, warm orange central trumpet, slightly crimped at the edges, with a marked green eye. Others in this group are *N.* 'Mint Julep' ♀ (42cm/17in), bright canary yellow, and *N.* 'Verona' ♀ (45cm/18in) with fluted cream blooms. *N.* 'Cheerfulness' ♀ (40cm/16in) is a 'double' variety with fragrant, pale creamy flowers; *N.* 'Panache' (40cm/16in) has white flowers that are amongst the largest (10cm/4in across) of the 'trumpet' group; *N. poeticus* 'Plenus' (30cm/12in) has sweetly fragrant, double white flowers.

BEST USES Plant through a spring border, in a raised bed and in woodland areas for spring colour; ideal for containers on a north-facing patio

FLOWERS April
SCENTED No
For cultivation, see *Narcissus* 'Dutch Master'

Narcissus 'Dutch Master' ♀
Daffodil

⬆ 45cm/18in ⬌ 10cm/4in   **EASY**

These upright bulbous perennials each produce one or more flowers in early spring, with narrow strap-like leaves appearing at the same time as the flowers. Leafless, smooth green stalks bear a six-petalled flower with a central trumpet. This popular, vigorous, classic variety has golden yellow blooms, with a distinctive flared, frilled trumpet of the same golden yellow. Other 'trumpet' varieties include *N.* 'Mount Hood' ♀ (42cm/17in), in parchment creamy yellow, and *N.* 'Spellbinder' ♀ (50cm/20in), yellow with pale yellow trumpets.

BEST USES 'Dutch Master' has a well-deserved reputation for vigorous reliability, so is ideal for the mixed spring border or naturalising in grassy areas

FLOWERS March to April
SCENTED No
ASPECT Any, in a sheltered or exposed position; full sun to partial shade
SOIL Any fertile, moist, humus-rich, well-drained soil
HARDINESS Fully hardy at temperatures down to -15°C/5°F; needs no winter protection
DROUGHT TOLERANCE Poor
PROBLEMS Narcissus bulb fly and narcissus eelworms; narcissus basal rot
CARE Plant bulbs to twice their depth in autumn; deadhead faded blooms, but leave foliage to die back naturally
PROPAGATION Division of large clumps after flowering when the leaves are browning

Omphalodes cappadocica 'Cherry Ingram'  Navelwort

⬆ 25cm/10in ⬌ 40cm/16in   **EASY**

This carpeting rhizomatous perennial woodlander from Turkey delivers simple elegance with masses of gentian blue flowers emerging above mounds of semi-evergreen heart-shaped leaves. This is one of the best, owing to the sheer brilliant blue of the larger than average flowers. It resents disturbance and is best in moist shade but is easy to care for once established, spreading itself around in all the right places. *O.c.* 'Starry Eyes' has sky blue flowers edged white; *O.c.* 'Parisian Skies' (25cm/10in) has clear, sky blue flowers.

BEST USES A pure and pretty plant that lends itself to many uses, in wildflower meadows, informal and tumbling cottage gardens, a shady corner of the garden or a woodland setting

FLOWERS March to April

SCENTED No

ASPECT East or west facing, in a sheltered position; partial shade

SOIL Any fertile, humus-rich, moist, well-drained soil

HARDINESS Fully hardy at temperatures down to -15°C/5°F; needs no winter protection

DROUGHT TOLERANCE Poor

PROBLEMS Slugs and snails; late frosts can damage leaves

CARE Mulch with organic matter in early spring to conserve moisture in the soil

PROPAGATION Self-seeds easily once established; division in spring

Podophyllum peltatum
American mandrake

⬆ 40cm/16in ⬌ Indefinite   **EASY**

Found in North America from Ontario to Texas in rich meadows and moist woodlands, this vigorous rhizomatous perennial has much to offer for damp shade. Mound-forming, glossy bright green, deeply cut leaves (the size of dinner plates) are held umbrella-like atop tall, smooth, straight stems. They show off large, drooping, simple, malodorous flowers that are waxy white, tinged pink, and are followed by oval yellowish fruits. They spread easily, making large swathes in no time. (Beware: both roots and leaves are extremely toxic.)

BEST USES Excellent for shady borders or woodland gardens; will thrive in dry shade if soil is improved with humus before planting and kept moist

FLOWERS April to June

SCENTED Unpleasantly scented flowers

ASPECT North, east or west facing, in a sheltered position; partial to full shade

SOIL Any fertile, moist, humus-rich, well-drained soil

HARDINESS Fully hardy at temperatures down to -15°C/5°F; needs no winter protection

DROUGHT TOLERANCE Poor

PROBLEMS Slugs and snails like to nibble young foliage; young leaves can be damaged by frost

CARE Mulch in spring

PROPAGATION Division in spring; sow ripe seed immediately in pots in a cold frame

PRIMULAS

Primula japonica 'Miller's Crimson'

⬆ 45cm/18in ⬌ 45cm/18in   MEDIUM

Primulas are an enormous group of plants (with over 500 species), originally from meadows, woodlands and mountains throughout the northern hemisphere. The tender bedding plants (known as polyanthus) provide invaluable early spring colour and wild primroses are ideal for naturalising in grassy areas. Taller herbaceous primulas (from 60cm/24in up to 1.2m/4ft) are better suited to flower borders or moist garden areas. Primulas prefer light shade and moist soil and tend to be short-lived, but many are easily grown from seed.

The compact, spring-flowering auriculas have been bred since the fifteenth century to give them their unique looks (the petals almost look hand painted) and colours. Some auricula flowers have a floury appearance ('*farina*'), but this is a desirable feature, not a fungal disease! They are often grown for exhibitions, but do well as garden plants in loam or clay soils and are useful for edging borders. *P. auricula* 'Astolat' (20cm/8in) is evergreen and has fragrant shallow flowers marked in banded circles of white, then red and green from the yellow centres.

P. 'Wanda' ♟ (10cm/4in) has deep purple-cerise flowers and red-tinted foliage; *P. rosea* 'Grandiflora' (20cm/8in) has deep rose pink flowers in spring; *P. denticulata* ♟ (50cm/20in) – *see above* – has purple drumstick globed flowers on straight leafless stems in spring and summer; *P.d.* var. *alba* is the white version; *P. beesiana* (60cm/24in) has reddy purple flowers in summer.

This lovely Japanese primula is not at all like the rainbow-coloured polyanthus that deluge garden centres in early spring. It is a 'candelabra' type, with whorled flowers set at intervals along a barish stem, and there are some cracking ones out there, making it very hard to choose just one. *P.j.* 'Miller's Crimson' offers broad mid-green leaves and deep, ruby red whorled flowers with even darker eyes, opening successively on straight stems in late spring. *P.j.* 'Postford White' ♟ has white flowers with golden centres; *P.j.* 'Carminea' has vivid fuchsia pink flowers; both are taller (up to 80cm/32in).

BEST USES Ideal at the pond or water's edge or as bold underplanting in moist (not boggy), shady areas of the garden; pleasing in the cottage garden amongst ferns and spring bulbs; grows successfully in moist containers

FLOWERS April to July

SCENTED No

ASPECT North, east or west facing, in a sheltered or exposed position; full sun to partial shade

SOIL Any fertile, humus-rich, moist soil

HARDINESS Fully hardy at temperatures down to -15°C/5°F; needs no winter protection

DROUGHT TOLERANCE Poor

PROBLEMS *Botrytis* (grey mould) and leaf spot

CARE Cut back spent flower stems

PROPAGATION Division in autumn to early spring

Primula vulgaris ♀
Wild primrose

⬆ 20cm/8in ⬌ 35cm/14in   **EASY**

This semi-evergreen native perennial, with its simple elegance, is instantly recognisable. Its coarse, oval, spoon-shaped, fresh green leaves, with etched veining, circle in rosette formation. From these low basal mounds grow short, softly bristled stems, each topped with sweetly fragrant, single, pale yellow flowers, up to 4cm/1½in across, with marked, darker yellow eyes. *P.v.* 'Alba Plena' is a lovely double-flowered white variety.

> **BEST USES** Ideal for the small cottage garden or a wildflower or woodland garden; a delightful addition in pots and in containers in north-facing gardens

FLOWERS March to May
SCENTED Scented flowers
ASPECT Any, in a sheltered position; partial to full shade
SOIL Any fertile, moist, well-drained soil
HARDINESS Fully hardy at temperatures down to -15°C/5°F; needs no winter protection
DROUGHT TOLERANCE Poor
PROBLEMS *Botrytis* (grey mould) and leaf spot
CARE Deadhead to prevent self-seeding
PROPAGATION Division every two years, to maintain flowering in late spring or autumn

Pulmonaria 'Sissinghurst White' ♀
Lungwort

⬆ 30cm/12in ⬌ 45cm/18in   **EASY**

The lungworts from south-east Europe are an incredibly useful group of deciduous and semi-evergreen plants, providing excellent ground cover effortlessly. This rhizomatous, semi-evergreen perennial forms neat, generous clumps of oval, mid-green leaves (up to 25cm/10in long), heavily spotted with white, from which emerge bristly green stems, flushed slightly damson, holding pale pink buds that open to snow white tubular flowers – a bit unusual as lungworts are generally purple and blue-flowering. *P.* 'Apple Frost' has pink flowers.

> **BEST USES** Ideal ground cover for slopes and banks; plant with spring bulbs in woodland or the wildflower garden; bees love it; deer and rabbit proof

FLOWERS March to April
SCENTED No
ASPECT North, east or west facing, in a sheltered or exposed position; partial to full shade
SOIL Any fertile, moist, humus-rich, well-drained soil
HARDINESS Fully hardy at temperatures down to -15°C/5°F; needs no winter protection
DROUGHT TOLERANCE Poor
PROBLEMS Slugs and snails; powdery mildew
CARE Mulch well with organic matter in spring to minimise fungal outbreaks; deadhead spent flowers to keep flowers true; remove tatty leaves after flowering to encourage new growth
PROPAGATION Division every 4–5 years in autumn; root cuttings in mid-winter

Pulsatilla vulgaris 'Röde Klokke'
Pasque flower

⬆ 20cm/8in ⬌ 20cm/8in   MEDIUM

Pasque flowers are deciduous perennials from western Europe that have attractive, ferny, soft green leaves and bear single, open bell-shaped, purple to white flowers that are incredibly pretty. This stunning variety has deep velvety red flowers with attractive golden eyes: the unusual colouring makes it one of the best of the spring bunch. More commonly available, *P. vulgaris* ♛ has mid-purple flowers, and *P.v.* 'Alba' has white flowers with golden stamens. (All parts of this plant are poisonous and can cause skin irritation.)

BEST USES Ideal in raised or alpine beds and containers; very effective studding the front of the flower border in spring

FLOWERS March to May
SCENTED No
ASPECT South, east or west facing, in an exposed or sheltered position; full sun to partial shade
SOIL Any fertile, gritty, well-drained, moist soil; dislikes sitting in winter wet
HARDINESS Fully hardy at temperatures down to -15°C/5°F; needs no winter protection
DROUGHT TOLERANCE Poor
PROBLEMS Slugs and snails like to nibble young foliage; resents disturbance
CARE Add a good shovelful of gravel or pea shingle to the planting hole and plant slightly on a mound to ensure sharp drainage
PROPAGATION Sow ripe seed immediately in pots in a cold frame; root cuttings in winter

Ranunculus aconitifolius 'Flore Pleno' ♛
White bachelor's buttons/Fair maids of Kent

⬆ 60cm/24in ⬌ 60cm/24in   EASY

Belonging to the buttercup family, this dainty, clump-forming perennial from central Europe possesses a quiet grace with attractive, large, lobed, glossy dark green leaves, rather like those of *Aconitum* (Monkshood), and branched stems of masses of small, creamy white pompom-like flowers with light green centres from late spring. Its airy flower heads set against the spring border are always charming and fairly long-lasting. (Its sap can cause skin irritation.)

BEST USES Lovely in the formal spring border and cottage garden alike; at home at the pond's edge or even in a woodland garden with spring-flowering bulbs and ferns; excellent as a cut flower

FLOWERS April to June
SCENTED No
ASPECT South, east or west facing, in a sheltered position; full sun to partial shade
SOIL Any fertile, moist, humus-rich, well-drained soil
HARDINESS Fully hardy at temperatures down to -15°C/5°F; needs no winter protection
DROUGHT TOLERANCE Poor
PROBLEMS Aphids, slugs and snails; powdery mildew
CARE Remove spent flower stems and cut back to ground level in late winter or early spring
PROPAGATION Division in spring or autumn

Saxifraga 'Cloth of Gold' (*exarta* subsp. *moschata*)

⬆ 10cm/4in ⬌ 30cm/12in   EASY

Saxifrages are cushioned or mat-forming perennials, some with mossy or silver foliage, that can be evergreen, semi-evergreen or deciduous, found in mountainous areas across the northern hemisphere (so they appreciate well-drained soil). There are more than 400 species within this family, with flowering from winter through to autumn. This slow-growing, mossy European variety forms neat, rounded hummocks of small, lobed, bright gold leaves, with short, barely noticeable stems, topped with a frenzy of star-shaped yellow-white flowers in spring.

BEST USES Perfect for the small cottage garden; a delightful addition in pots or troughs; ideal dotted through a gravel garden

FLOWERS March to May
SCENTED No
ASPECT Any, in a sheltered or exposed position; full sun to partial shade
SOIL Any fertile, humus-rich, moist, well-drained soil
HARDINESS Fully hardy at temperatures down to -15°C/5°F; needs no winter protection
DROUGHT TOLERANCE Poor
PROBLEMS Won't tolerate drought or hot, humid weather
CARE Trim lightly after flowering
PROPAGATION Detach rooted rosettes and pot up as new plants; sow seed in pots in a cold frame in autumn

Sisyrinchium 'E.K. Balls'

⬆ 25cm/10in ⬌ 15cm/6in   EASY

This semi-evergreen rhizomatous perennial of American origin is a garden hybrid and has stiff, grass-like leaves forming sculptural fans (a bit like gladioli to look at), with smooth, green leafless stems, each topped with a succession of flower buds that open to display five-petalled, star-shaped, deep rich blue flowers, with golden eyes, from early summer. Although this is billed as semi-evergreen, the leaves take a hammering and can be cut back once they are past their best. The blue flowers are unusual: sisyrinchium flowers generally come in shades of yellow.

BEST USES Ideal as an architectural plant in a sunny border; equally suited to a Mediterranean or cottage garden

FLOWERS May to June
SCENTED No
ASPECT South or west facing, in a sheltered or exposed position; full sun
SOIL Any fertile, humus-rich, well-drained soil
HARDINESS Fully hardy at temperatures down to -15°C/5°F; needs no winter protection
DROUGHT TOLERANCE Good, once established (in extended drought will die back until next year)
PROBLEMS None
CARE Cut back faded flowers and tatty foliage
PROPAGATION Division in spring

Tiarella wherryi 🏅
Foam flower

⬆ 20cm/8in ⬌ 15cm/6in   **EASY**

We have the USA to thank for this graceful, clump-forming herbaceous perennial with its discreet tri-lobed purple-tinged green leaves and smooth, purple-flushed stems, carrying airy spires of pinky white flowers. It's pretty unfussy about soil and I can't think of a plant that can enhance a shady garden quite so effortlessly from late spring until mid-summer. *T.w.* 'Bronze Beauty' has unusual maple-like leaves tinted red-bronze with pale pink flowers.

> **BEST USES** Ideal for the shady flower border; attractive as ground cover, planted in drifts in woodland areas or spring flower borders

FLOWERS May to July
SCENTED No
ASPECT North, east or west facing, in a sheltered position, protected from excessive winter wet; partial to full shade
SOIL Any fertile, well-drained, moist, humus-rich soil
HARDINESS Fully hardy at temperatures down to -15°C/5°F; needs no winter protection
DROUGHT TOLERANCE Poor
PROBLEMS Slugs and snails
CARE Remove spent flower heads; mulch the base generously with organic matter in spring
PROPAGATION Division in spring; sow ripe seed immediately in pots in a cold frame

Trollius × cultorum 'Alabaster'
Globeflower

⬆ 60cm/24in ⬌ 40cm/16in   **EASY**

This gorgeous clump-forming perennial for damp places comes from Asia and Europe, and has finely toothed mid-green leaves and tall, slender, smooth stems, each topped with dainty, cupped, pale lemony white flowers (up to 5cm/2in across) in spring. You may have to search around for this particular variety as it is on every discerning gardener's wish list and seems to sell out, but it is worth the effort. *T. × c.* 'Earliest of All' bears golden yellow flowers; *T. × c.* 'Lemon Queen' has cool lemon flowers.

> **BEST USES** Gorgeous in the bog garden or in a moist, shady wildflower or cottage garden

FLOWERS April to June
SCENTED No
ASPECT South, east or west facing, in a sheltered or exposed position; full sun to partial shade
SOIL Any fertile, moist, well-drained soil
HARDINESS Fully hardy at temperatures down to -15°C/5°F; needs no winter protection
DROUGHT TOLERANCE Poor
PROBLEMS Powdery mildew
CARE Cut back spent flowering stems hard to encourage a second flush of flowers
PROPAGATION Division as new growth starts in spring or after flowering in summer

GREENFINGER TIP *This can be slow to establish and propagation can be difficult: give it ideal growing conditions and be patient*

Tulipa 'Green Wave'
Tulip

⬆ 60cm/24in ⬌ 10cm/4in   **EASY**

Tulips are bulbous perennials from Europe to Asia, with broad, lax, strappy, mid-green leaves and single straight, smooth green stems, bearing single or clustered six-petalled flowers, which are generally cupped or goblet-shaped, in almost every colour of the rainbow. They range in height from 8cm/3in up to 60cm/24in, and tend to dwindle rather than increase over the years. 'Parrot' tulips, of which this is one, are recognised by their frilled, ruffled or fringed blooms and often have marked striping to the petals. This lovely variety has large, deep green flower buds, with white-stained edges, that open to very large, extravagant ruffled flowers of the palest apple green, flushed pastel pink at the frilled edges. Other choice parrot varieties (and there are many) include the shaggy-edged white flowers, stained pale green, of *T.* 'White Parrot' (40cm/16in); the deep purple-black of *T.* 'Black Parrot' ♓ and the peachy apricot-fringed blooms, with cream striping, of *T.* 'Apricot Parrot' ♓ (both 50cm/20in); and the dusky blood red of *T.* 'Rococo' (35cm/14in).

BEST USES A joyful addition to cottage gardens and formal borders; does well in containers for city gardeners; great as cut flowers (push a pin through the bottom of the flower stalks to stop them swooning in the vase)

FLOWERS May
SCENTED No
For cultivation, see *Tulipa* 'Queen of Night'

Tulipa 'Queen of Night'
Tulip

⬆ 60cm/24in ⬌ 10cm/4cm   **EASY**

'Queen of Night' is a Single Late tulip, with grey-green strap-like leaves and tall, straight stems topped with single sumptuous, deep chocolate-plum-coloured cupped flowers with white stamens. *T.* 'Pink Diamond' (also Single Late) is pale shell pink; *T.* 'Diana' (28cm/11in) (Single Early) has single pure white flowers in mid-spring; *T.* 'Apeldoorn' (60cm/24in) (Darwin Hybrid) has bright red flowers in mid-spring; *T.* 'Angélique' ♓ (30cm/12in) (Double Late) has loose, double, pale pink flowers, flushed pale green at the base, in late spring; *T.* 'Mount Tacoma' (40cm/16in) (Double Late) has double, creamy white flowers in late spring.

BEST USES Happy in containers or in a formal or cottage garden flower border; very effective for adding blocks of colour to a formal planting scheme

FLOWERS April to May
SCENTED No
ASPECT South or west facing, in a sheltered or exposed position; full sun
SOIL Any fertile, well-drained soil
HARDINESS Fully hardy at temperatures down to -15°C/5°F; needs no winter protection
DROUGHT TOLERANCE Poor
PROBLEMS Eelworms, slugs and snails; tulip fire
CARE Deadhead faded flowers, allowing stems to die back naturally; plant bulbs 15cm/6in deep in autumn
PROPAGATION Pot up offsets in summer and grow on for 1–2 years before planting out

Veronica umbrosa 'Georgia Blue'
(formerly *V. peduncularis* 'Oxford Blue')

⬆ 10cm/4in ⬌ 60cm/24in+   **EASY**

A mat-forming evergreen perennial from Turkey that flowers earlier than some of the taller varieties, this veronica has a vigorous, creeping, prostrate habit with branching stems and attractive serrated green leaves (up to 2.5cm/1in long) that redden in autumn to winter. However, it is the profusion of dainty, saucer-shaped sky blue flowers with white eyes that are its main attraction. Flowering so early in the year, it's a breath of cheer at the end of winter and a tough little contender, bearing drought and wet with equal fortitude and sending out unexpected blooms in summer or sometimes even autumn.

> **BEST USES** Perfect at the front of a border; enjoys semi-shade conditions under shrubs or in a mixed border; does well in containers in a shady courtyard or city patio

FLOWERS February to April
SCENTED No
ASPECT Any, in a sheltered position; full sun to partial shade
SOIL Any fertile, humus-rich, moist, well-drained soil
HARDINESS Fully hardy at temperatures down to -15°C/5°F; needs no winter protection
DROUGHT TOLERANCE Poor
PROBLEMS Powdery mildew
CARE Mulch annually with organic matter
PROPAGATION Division in spring or autumn; sow seed in pots in a cold frame in autumn

Viola sororia 'Freckles'

⬆ 10cm/4in ⬌ 30cm/12in   **EASY**

Members of the viola family are largely hardy, evergreen perennials from temperate regions worldwide and include the ever-popular cottage garden pansies and violets. *V.s.* 'Freckles' is a pretty, mound-forming, short-lived, rhizomatous herbaceous perennial, with dark green rounded leaves and short, upright spurs bearing very dainty, simple, four-petalled flowers that are white, tinted blue, spotted with purple freckles. *V.s.* 'Albiflora' ♀ has evergreen foliage and pure white flowers from April to June; the dark form *V.s.* 'Priceana' (20cm/8in) has white flowers with deep mauve veins from February to May.

> **BEST USES** No self-respecting cottage garden will be without this plant; does well in containers or in a border; always a good choice for edging borders

FLOWERS March to May
SCENTED No
ASPECT South, east or west facing, in a sheltered or exposed position; full sun to partial shade
SOIL Any fertile, moist, well-drained soil
HARDINESS Fully hardy at temperatures down to -15°C/5°F; needs no winter protection
DROUGHT TOLERANCE Poor
PROBLEMS Slugs and snails; powdery mildew
CARE Deadhead faded blooms to prolong flowering
PROPAGATION Division in spring

Anthericum liliago 'Major' 🏅
St Bernard's lily

⬆ 90cm/3ft ⬌ 50cm/20in   **EASY**

This rhizomatous herbaceous perennial from the southern Mediterranean forms clumps of tough, long, narrow grey-green leaves. In mid-spring to summer (and often later than this) it sends up numerous wiry, wand-like stems with tubular star-shaped white flowers that open sequentially from the bottom up. After flowering, brown seed heads appear. It is a graceful, airy plant that seems to sell out fast, though there are quite a few nurseries that stock it. *A. liliago* has smaller white flowers.

> **BEST USES** Delightful in a cottage garden, gravel or Mediterranean garden; try planting with shorter ornamental grasses, echinacea, *Verbena bonariensis* and angelica; bees love it

FLOWERS April to June
SCENTED No
ASPECT South, east or west facing, in a sheltered or exposed position; full sun
SOIL Any fertile, humus-rich, well-drained soil
HARDINESS Fully hardy at temperatures down to -15°C/5°F; needs no winter protection
DROUGHT TOLERANCE Poor
PROBLEMS Slugs and snails like to nibble the young spring growth
CARE Remove spent flower stems to prevent self-seeding; mulch annually in spring
PROPAGATION Division in spring

Anthriscus sylvestris 'Ravenswing'
Purple cow parsley

⬆ 90cm/3ft ⬌ 30cm/12in   **EASY**

Europe has brought us some lovely garden plants and this is a plummy version of our native cow parsley (commonly sighted on roadsides and hedgerows, and pretty invasive). This informal, airy variety can be grown as a clump-forming biennial or short-lived perennial and has tall, graceful stems with finely cut, deep claret leaves and tall stems topped with cloud-like sprays of diminutive white flowers from spring to early summer. It does well in poor soils, but adding organic matter enormously improves its ability to cope with drought.

> **BEST USES** Associates well with spring bulbs, looking quite at home in a cottage garden or more formal border; excellent for underplanting in shrub borders; ideal for wildlife havens and rough, grassy areas around ponds, as insects love it

FLOWERS May to July
SCENTED No
ASPECT South, east or west facing, in a sheltered or exposed position; full sun to partial shade
SOIL Any fertile, well-drained soil
HARDINESS Fully hardy at temperatures down to -15°C/5°F; needs no winter protection
DROUGHT TOLERANCE Good, once established
PROBLEMS Slugs and snails may damage young growth; powdery mildew
CARE Cut back flower stems after flowering
PROPAGATION Self-seeds easily; sow seed in final flowering position in spring

Aquilegia vulgaris var. *stellata* 'Nora Barlow' (Barlow Series) ♟

⬆ 90cm/3ft ↔ 50cm/20in   **EASY**

Commonly known as Columbine or Granny's bonnet, this herbaceous perennial is found in mountainous and meadow areas of the northern hemisphere. Versatile and promiscuous, they self-seed freely and are easily spotted by their dainty, nodding, spurred flowers, in shades of purple, yellow, pink, white and blue, and appealing lobed foliage. This variety has attractive, deeply divided grey-green foliage, bearing dainty, nodding, double, dark pink flowers, suffused with soft pink, in late spring. *A.v.* 'Nivea' ♟ has pure white single-spurred flowers; *A.v.* 'William Guiness' has purple-black and white single-spurred flowers.

> **BEST USES** Ideal for the cottage or informal garden; colonise rapidly in woodland gardens, for effective ground cover; terrific in rough grass

FLOWERS May to June
SCENTED No
ASPECT Any, in a sheltered or exposed position; full sun to partial shade
SOIL Any fertile, well-drained soil
HARDINESS Fully hardy at temperatures down to -15°C/5°F; needs no winter protection
DROUGHT TOLERANCE Good, once established
PROBLEMS Powdery mildew
CARE Deadhead to prevent self-seeding; cut spent flowers back to the mound of basal leaves
PROPAGATION Self-seeds easily; division of named varieties in spring (slow to re-establish); sow seed in pots in a cold frame in autumn

Asphodelus albus Asphodel/King's spear

⬆ 90cm/3ft ↔ 30cm/12in   **EASY**

Originally from meadows, woodlands and scrub lands from the Himalayas to the Mediterranean, this lovely rhizomatous perennial is quite often overlooked. It has long, grassy, mid-green leaves and carries star-shaped white flowers, each petal marked with a single, muted copper stripe, and spidery cream stamens. The flowers gradually open from the bottom up on tall, slender stems, in late spring to early summer. Related to the lily family, it will tolerate dry conditions and is very low maintenance, only asking for deep, reasonably fertile soil to thrive.

> **BEST USES** Adds elegant vertical accents to the cottage garden, formal border or gravel garden; beautiful naturalised amongst swaying grasses

FLOWERS May to June
SCENTED No
ASPECT South, east or west facing, in a sheltered position; full sun
SOIL Any fertile, well-drained soil
HARDINESS Fully hardy at temperatures down to -15°C/5°F; needs no winter protection
DROUGHT TOLERANCE Good, once established
PROBLEMS Aphids
CARE May need staking; remove dead flower stems in late autumn
PROPAGATION Division in early spring; sow seed in pots in a cold frame in spring

Dicentra spectabilis 🏅
Bleeding heart

⬆ 90cm/3ft ⬌ 45cm/18in   **EASY**

A beautiful, if ephemeral, perennial plant from Asia making mounds of attractive, fresh, ferny green leaves with slender, smooth, arching pink stems bearing tremulous, heart-shaped rose-coloured lockets with pinky white teardrops dangling from the bottom of the flowers. The white variety *D.s.* 'Alba' 🏅 is also very pretty.

> **BEST USES** Delightful in the middle of a border or in a lightly shaded woodland garden; its appearance is fleeting so plant with hardy geraniums or leafy plants to fill the gap after it has faded; does well in a sunny border if the soil is kept reliably moist

FLOWERS May to June
SCENTED No
ASPECT Any, in a sheltered position; full sun to partial shade
SOIL Any fertile, humus-rich, well-drained soil
HARDINESS Fully hardy at temperatures down to -15°C/5°F; needs no winter protection
DROUGHT TOLERANCE Poor
PROBLEMS Slugs and snails like to nibble the young spring growth
CARE Cut back to ground level in autumn
PROPAGATION Division of large clumps in early spring or early autumn, after the leaves have died back; sow seed in spring; root cuttings in winter

Doronicum × excelsum 'Harpur Crewe'
Leopard's bane

⬆ 75cm/30in ⬌ 30cm/12in   **EASY**

European doronicums are clump-forming, rhizomatous herbaceous perennials that have a reputation for thuggery and can be invasive, but this robust hybrid is more restrained than some of its counterparts. Doronicums are easy-to-grow plants that do best in moist ground but are happy in a wide range of soils if kept well watered. The heart-shaped mid-green leaves narrow further up the stem, and branching stems are topped off with large, flat-headed, cheerful daisy-like flowers that give a much needed dash of sunshine yellow in early spring. If you are short of space, opt for the gold-flowered *D.* 'Little Leo' (30cm/12in).

> **BEST USES** Ideal for early colour in the spring border; does well in coastal areas and in containers

FLOWERS April to May
SCENTED No
ASPECT Any, in a sheltered position; partial shade
SOIL Any fertile, moisture-retentive soil
HARDINESS Fully hardy at temperatures down to -15°C/5°F; needs no winter protection
DROUGHT TOLERANCE Poor
PROBLEMS Powdery mildew
CARE Cut down to ground level in autumn; mulch well in winter to conserve moisture; taller varieties benefit from staking
PROPAGATION Division after flowering

Maianthemum racemosum 🏅
(formerly *Smilacina racemosa*)

⬆ 90cm/3ft ⬌ 45cm/18in   **EASY**

Unusually tall for a spring perennial, this rhizomatous clump-forming plant from Mexico has incredibly appealing, arching, lightly ribbed, oval, leathery apple green leaves, which tone down to green-gold in autumn. It's very similar in appearance to *Polygonatum odoratum* (Solomon's seal), but the similarity ends once you see the flowers: upright, fluffy, creamy white plumes (15cm/6in long), in late spring, followed by cream-coloured berries that turn a rich red in autumn. The fragrant flowers are sweetly lemon-scented.

> **BEST USES** Ideal for woodland or a shady corner of the garden; provides effective ground cover and looks fabulous planted with ferns and spring bulbs

FLOWERS May to June
SCENTED Yes
ASPECT North, east or west facing, in a sheltered position, with protection from cold winds; partial to full shade
SOIL Any fertile, moist, humus-rich soil; prefers neutral to acid soil
HARDINESS Fully hardy at temperatures down to -15°C/5°F; needs no winter protection
DROUGHT TOLERANCE Poor
PROBLEMS Slugs and snails
CARE Remove the spent flower heads; mulch annually with organic matter
PROPAGATION Division in spring; sow ripe seed in pots in a cold frame in autumn

Paeonia 'Claire de Lune'
Peony

⬆ 80cm/32in ⬌ 70cm/28in   **EASY**

Peonies are tuberous, clump-forming perennials from Europe and Asia, grown for their gorgeous flowers. This extravagant variety has deeply cut deep green leaves and smooth red stems, bearing very large, fat flower buds that open to highly fragrant, double, white flowers, tinted with palest pink at the base if you look carefully, and dense golden stamens. It flowers earlier than many other varieties: peonies are generally at their flowering best in June.

> **BEST USES** This variety is excellent for bridging the transition from spring to early summer: the handsome foliage clumps up spectacularly well and is an attractive feature in its own right

FLOWERS May to June
SCENTED Yes
ASPECT South, east or west facing, in a sheltered or exposed position; full sun to partial shade
SOIL Any fertile, humus-rich, well-drained soil
HARDINESS Fully hardy at temperatures down to -15°C/5°F; needs no winter protection
DROUGHT TOLERANCE Poor
PROBLEMS Eelworms; *Botrytis* (grey mould) and peony wilt
CARE May need staking; deadhead spent flowers; mulch the base in spring
PROPAGATION Division in autumn or spring; root cuttings in winter

Polygonatum odoratum ♈
Solomon's seal

⬆ 85cm/34in ⬌ 30cm/12in EASY

One of my favourite plants, Solomon's seal is a rhizomatous perennial found as far afield as Japan, Russia and Europe. It has handsome arching stems of smooth, fresh green leaves and fragrant white-tipped tubular flowers in late spring, hanging from smooth stems like teardrops. These are followed by inedible round black berries. It spreads by creeping rhizomes, so new plants are easily had. There's few to match it for possessing the big three: flower, foliage and fragrance. No garden should be without it. The unusual double-flowered form *P.o.* 'Flore Pleno' ♈ is also a must-have. (All parts of the plant are toxic.)

> **BEST USES** This plant is happy in a woodland garden or shady setting; looks stunning planted with ferns, foxgloves and hardy geraniums

FLOWERS May
SCENTED Yes
ASPECT Any, in a sheltered position; partial to full shade
SOIL Any fertile, moist, humus-rich, well-drained soil
HARDINESS Fully hardy at temperatures down to -15°C/5°F; needs no winter protection
DROUGHT TOLERANCE Poor
PROBLEMS Sawfly larvae, slugs and snails
CARE Mulch in spring; cut back leaves in autumn
PROPAGATION Division as new growth starts in spring

Tellima grandiflora
Fringe cups

⬆ 80cm/32in ⬌ 30cm/12in EASY

From North America, this clump-forming herbaceous perennial has very attractive heart-shaped, scalloped, fresh green leaves (up to 10cm/4in across) and tall upright stems, bearing spikes of tightly closed buds that open to small, lightly scented, greenish white, bell-shaped flowers in late spring to early summer. A reliable doer in dry shade, it will put up with a wide range of soil conditions and self-seeds with ease. *T.g.* Rubra Group has creamy pinkish flowers, with burgundy-tinted leaves in winter; *T.g.* Odorata Group has fragrant creamy flowers and apple green leaves.

> **BEST USES** Modest but invaluable in a cottage garden or under shrubs; reliable ground cover in the woodland garden; foliage combines beautifully with hostas, dark-coloured hardy geraniums and ferns

FLOWERS May to July
SCENTED Yes
ASPECT South, east or west facing, in a sheltered position; full sun to partial shade
SOIL Any fertile, humus-rich, well-drained soil; tolerant of dry conditions
HARDINESS Fully hardy at temperatures down to -15°C/5°F; needs no winter protection
DROUGHT TOLERANCE Medium, once established
PROBLEMS Slugs and snails
CARE Remove spent flower heads; mulch in spring
PROPAGATION Division in spring; sow ripe seed immediately in pots in a cold frame

Uvularia grandiflora ♟
Bellwort

⬆ 75cm/30in ⬌ 30cm/12in   EASY

This North American woodlander is an upright, clump-forming rhizomatous herbaceous perennial, with creeping rootstock, but is slow to spread. Known in the USA as Merrybells, it has fresh green, drooping, lance-shaped leaves on slightly arching stems, framing clusters of pendent, narrow, bell-shaped yellow flowers that are flushed green at the base. It is a bit of a rarity and should be grown more commonly, as it is a real dash of cheer in spring.

BEST USES Ideal for the woodland or wildlife garden and invaluable in a spring border; does well in containers in a shady corner

FLOWERS April to June

SCENTED No

ASPECT North, east or west facing, in a sheltered position; partial to full shade

SOIL Any fertile, moist, humus-rich soil

HARDINESS Fully hardy at temperatures down to -15°C/5°F; needs no winter protection

DROUGHT TOLERANCE Poor

PROBLEMS Slugs and snails

CARE Mulch the base with leafmould or organic matter in early spring to preserve moisture in the soil, as this plant will not tolerate any dryness

PROPAGATION Division in spring

Zantedeschia aethiopica 'Crowborough' ♟ Arum lily

⬆ 90cm/3ft ⬌ 50cm/20in   MEDIUM

Originating in swamplands and moist soils in South Africa, these rhizomatous perennials are reliably evergreen in warm climates (in cold regions the foliage will die back completely), normally flowering in summer. This clump-forming, upright variety throws up its flowers earlier than other varieties, in late spring to early summer, and has arrow-shaped, glossy, deep green leaves and pure, slightly waxy white spathed flowers (up to 15cm/6in across). *Z.a.* 'Green Goddess' ♟ has marbled green and lime-coloured spathes, flowering in summer.

BEST USES The sculptural flower shape and fine foliage make this excellent for chic city gardens as well as formal beds and borders; good in large, well watered pots or by the water's edge

FLOWERS May to June

SCENTED No

ASPECT South, east or west facing, in a sheltered position; full sun

SOIL Any fertile, moisture-retentive, damp or boggy soil

HARDINESS Frost hardy/borderline at temperatures down to -5°C/23°F; may need winter protection in colder areas

DROUGHT TOLERANCE Poor

PROBLEMS Aphids

CARE Protect the crown with a dry winter mulch in cold areas; don't allow to dry out

PROPAGATION Division in early spring

Acanthus spinosus L. ♟

Bear's breeches

⬆ 1.5m/5ft ⬌ 90cm/3ft   **EASY**

This architectural perennial from Italy and Turkey is worth growing for its large, handsome, glossy, deeply jagged leaves (90cm/3ft), which look good nine months of the year, and has the added bonus of long-lasting, tall, erect, plum-hooded flower spikes, marked white, rising like statuesque cathedral spires from the foliage in late spring to summer. It is not fussy about soil as long as it is well drained, and can cope with light shade, but it needs plenty of space and may become invasive.

BEST USES Makes an excellent focal point and adds year-round interest to the formal flower border; it is drought tolerant, and is shown off to full advantage in the barer spaces of a Mediterranean or gravel garden; goat and deer proof

FLOWERS May to July
SCENTED No
ASPECT Any, in a sheltered or exposed position; full sun to partial shade
SOIL Any fertile, well-drained soil
HARDINESS Fully hardy at temperatures down to -15°C/5°F; needs no winter protection
DROUGHT TOLERANCE Excellent, once established
PROBLEMS Slugs and snails nibble young foliage; powdery mildew
CARE Remove spent flower heads; cut to ground level in late winter or early spring
PROPAGATION Division in autumn or spring; root cuttings in winter

Darmera peltata ♟

Umbrella plant/Indian rhubarb

⬆ 2m/6ft ⬌ 90cm/3ft   **EASY**

This terrific rhizomatous herbaceous perennial from woodland and watersides in the USA has tall, hairy stems with huge (45cm/18in across), scalloped, rhubarb-like dark green leaves that flush a vivid ruby red in autumn. As if that wasn't enough, it bears umbrella-like flower clusters of gappy petalled white flowers, tinged pink, from spring to early summer. This can be invasive, so plant where it won't become a potential nuisance. *D.p.* 'Nana' (60cm/24in) is more compact.

BEST USES Dramatic as a sculptural plant at the water's edge or in a bog garden; ideal in awkward, damp borders; great for wildlife areas, attracting hoverflies, bees and butterflies

FLOWERS April to June
SCENTED No
ASPECT North, south or west facing, in a sheltered or exposed position; full sun to partial shade
SOIL Reliably moist, marshy or boggy soils
HARDINESS Fully hardy at temperatures down to -15°C/5°F; needs no winter protection
DROUGHT TOLERANCE Poor
PROBLEMS None
CARE Remove spent flower stems
PROPAGATION Division in spring; sow seed in pots in a cold frame in spring or autumn

GREENFINGER TIP *Avoid planting this in an east-facing spot as the flowers can get spoiled by frosts*

SUMMER

Nothing beats a summer's day; the morning dew steams in idle, curling wisps as a saffron sun creeps over the flagstones to warm the rich brown earth and entice fat flower buds to yield their extravagant blooms. So many gorgeous border plants are at their very best in the summer months, transforming your garden into a haven for butterflies and bees and displaying a never-ending pageantry of colour and scents for the sensuous gardener.

Alchemilla mollis 🏅
Lady's mantle

⬆ 60cm/24in ⬌ 75cm/30in   **EASY**

I cannot recommend this herbaceous perennial from Turkey highly enough: it earns its stripes again and again. Morning dew jewels the pleasing clumps of softly scalloped apple green leaves, and profuse sprays of acid yellow flowers are held high above the mounded leaves in summer. It tolerates a wide variety of soils and conditions, including difficult dry spots, is idiot-proof to grow and self-seeds with fair abundance. *A.m.* 'Thriller' (50cm/20in) is slightly more compact, with grey-green foliage and straw-coloured flowers.

BEST USES Excellent ground cover as it self-seeds so freely; lovely edging a border in both cottage and contemporary gardens; good as cut flowers

FLOWERS June to September
SCENTED No
ASPECT Any, in a sheltered or exposed position; full sun to partial shade
SOIL Any fertile, well-drained soil
HARDINESS Fully hardy at temperatures down to -15°C/5°F; needs no winter protection
DROUGHT TOLERANCE Good, once established
PROBLEMS None
CARE Cut back spent flowers to encourage new leaf growth and prevent over-zealous self-seeding; cut dead leaves back to ground level in late winter or spring
PROPAGATION Division in early spring or autumn; dig up and replant self-sown seedlings; sow seed in pots in a cold frame in spring

Allium 'Globemaster' ♙

⬆ 30cm/12in ⬌ 30cm/12in   **EASY**

Alliums are clump-forming bulbous perennials, related to the onion, hence the oniony smell when the leaves are bruised. This variety has smooth, strappy, lax greyish green leaves, but nobody gives a fig about the foliage. Held aloft on very sturdy, erect, smooth, straight self-supporting stems are large, showy puffballs of deep purple flowers (some 20cm/8in across) that really command attention. Each ball is made up of numerous tiny, star-shaped flowers. When the flowers fade, appealing skeletal seed heads are left behind. *A. giganteum* ♙ (1.5m/5ft) is taller but looks very similar, with smaller purple flower heads (10cm/4in across).

BEST USES Adds vertical interest to a border; attracts its fair share of bees and butterflies; ideal for wildflower, cottage or Mediterranean gardens

FLOWERS July

SCENTED Aromatic leaves, when crushed

ASPECT South, east or west facing, in a sheltered position; full sun

SOIL Any fertile, well-drained soil

HARDINESS Fully hardy at temperatures down to -15°C/5°F; needs no winter protection

DROUGHT TOLERANCE Good, once established

PROBLEMS Onion fly; downy mildew, onion white rot and powdery mildew

CARE Remove faded flowers after flowering (or leave to form skeletal seed heads)

PROPAGATION Division of bulblets in autumn

Allium sphaerocephalon

⬆ 60cm/24in ⬌ 8cm/3in   **EASY**

Alliums are bulbous perennials, from as far afield as Asia, Africa and Europe, and are members of the onion family. This modest variety has strappy, narrow foliage and tall, thin, bare stems, making elegant drumsticks of dense, claret-coloured flowers that are flushed green at the base as they flower. *A. unifolium* ♙ (30cm/12in) is a smaller, chive-like variety with star-shaped pale pink flowers from May to July.

BEST USES Adds vertical accents to formal or informal flower borders, rising from low leafy plantings; combines well with ornamental grasses; ideal for the wildflower garden, being loved by bees

FLOWERS July to August

SCENTED Aromatic leaves, when crushed

ASPECT South, east or west facing, in a sheltered position; full sun

SOIL Any fertile, well-drained soil

HARDINESS Fully hardy at temperatures down to -15°C/5°F; needs no winter protection

DROUGHT TOLERANCE Good, once established

PROBLEMS Onion fly; downy mildew, onion white rot and powdery mildew

CARE Cut back faded flowers in late winter or early spring

PROPAGATION Division of bulblets in autumn

Astrantia 'Hadspen Blood'
Masterwort

⬆ 50cm/20in ↔ 45cm/18in   **EASY**

Astrantia, a clump-forming herbaceous perennial from Europe, is amongst my top ten border perennials: it forms leafy clumps, the architectural flowers are lovely and reasonably long-flowering, and it is low maintenance. This variety has lobed, deep green leaves, edged in charcoal, and the characteristic pincushion-like deep burgundy flowers are held high above the leaves on slender, graceful stems. *A. major* 'Ruby Wedding' (90cm/3ft) is a taller variety, with deep wine red flowers; the gorgeous ragged flowers of *A.m.* subsp. *involucrata* 'Shaggy' ♀ (90cm/3ft) are white tipped green.

BEST USES Works equally well in the cottage garden, formal border or by the pond; also good for coastal conditions; excellent as a cut or dried flower

FLOWERS June to August

SCENTED No

ASPECT South, east or west facing, in a sheltered position; full sun to partial shade

SOIL Any fertile, moist, humus-rich, well-drained soil

HARDINESS Fully hardy at temperatures down to -15°C/5°F; needs no winter protection

DROUGHT TOLERANCE Poor

PROBLEMS Slugs and snails; powdery mildew

CARE Cut back flowering stems to ground level in early spring or autumn

PROPAGATION Division in spring; sow ripe seed immediately in pots in a cold frame

CAMPANULAS
Bellflower

Campanulas are a family of summer-flowering annuals, biennials and perennials found across southern Europe and Turkey, in meadows, rocky hillsides and woodlands, so they will put up with a wide variety of garden situations and are incredibly reliable performers. They come in shades of blue, lavender and white, with the occasional pink variety, and include small alpines as well as medium and tall border plants. The perennials like a well-drained sunny spot (although some appreciate partial shade) and are incredibly easy to grow.

The diminutive alpine varieties (10–30cm/4–12in) are perfect for rockeries or crammed into nooks and crannies in walls and paving, in containers or as flowering ground cover, from early summer, sometimes up to the first frosts. *C.* 'Birch Hybrid' ♀ (10cm/4in) is a non-invasive, evergreen variety flowering in summer; *C. carpatica* 'Blue Moonlight' has pretty, pale blue flowers in early to mid-summer.

The tall border campanulas (from 60cm/24in up to 1.5m/5ft) are elegant plants, largely flowering in summer. *C. latifolia* 'Brantwood' (75cm/30in) has sultry, deep violet, clustered belled flowers on self-supporting stems in early summer; *C. latiloba* 'Hidcote Amethyst' ♀ (75cm/30in), with lilac-pink bell flowers, and the white variety *C.l.* 'Alba' ♀ (90cm/3ft) both flower from summer to early autumn; *C.* 'Kent Belle' ♀ (1.5m/5ft) – *see above* – has sumptuous purple flowers from early to late summer.

Campanula 'Burghaltii' ♀

⬆ 35cm/14in ⬌ 40cm/16in   **EASY**

I have an enduring fondness for this clump-forming, rhizomatous campanula, with its heart-shaped fresh green leaves, simply because it enjoys a longer than average flowering period. It bears pretty, drooping, bell-shaped pale lavender flowers held on thin, arching stems through the summer, has a brief break, and then obligingly flowers on into mid-autumn.

BEST USES Perfect for the cottage garden, fronting a formal border or edging raised beds and pathways

FLOWERS June to October

SCENTED No

ASPECT Any, in a sheltered or exposed position; full sun to partial shade

SOIL Any fertile, moist, well-drained soil

HARDINESS Fully hardy at temperatures down to -15°C/5°F; needs no winter protection

DROUGHT TOLERANCE Poor

PROBLEMS Slugs and snails

CARE May need staking to support the abundant flowers; cut back spent flowers to encourage a modest second flush of flowering

PROPAGATION Division in autumn or spring; basal stem cuttings in spring

Campanula glomerata 'Superba' ♀
Clustered bellflower

⬆ 60cm/24in ⬌ Indefinite   **EASY**

Found as far afield as Asia to Europe, this clump-forming rhizomatous perennial has much to recommend it. It is strong-growing and masses up quite quickly (making an enviable clump within three years) and has hairy, lance-shaped mid-green leaves, with tall, straight, sturdy, bristly stems topped with dense, richly coloured deep purple clusters of bell-shaped flowers which prove irresistible to bees. *C.g.* var. *alba* (50cm/20in) has white flowers; the dwarf *C.g.* 'Purple Pixie', with deep purple flowers, is only 30cm/12in tall.

BEST USES An obvious choice for the cottage garden, though it is quite stately so would enhance a formal flower border equally well; adapts well to woodland planting, for those with a dappled spot

FLOWERS June to July

SCENTED No

ASPECT South, east or west facing, in a sheltered position; full sun to partial shade

SOIL Any fertile, moist, well-drained soil

HARDINESS Fully hardy at temperatures down to -15°C/5°F; needs no winter protection

DROUGHT TOLERANCE Poor

PROBLEMS Powdery mildew

CARE Remove faded flowers to encourage a second show

PROPAGATION Division in spring or autumn

Chaenorhinum origanifolium 'Blue Dream' Dwarf snapdragon

⬆ 20cm/8in ⬌ 30cm/12in   **EASY**

This dwarf, mat-forming herbaceous perennial can be found across the Mediterranean in dry, stony soils (so will be happy in new gardens built on builder's rubble). It has small, rounded grey-green leaves and lax stems that are smothered in tiny, pretty, purple snapdragon-like flowers, with pale yellow throats flushed white, all summer long. It spreads by runners. I believe there is a new pink version *C.o.* 'Pink Dream', with much the same height, habit and spread.

BEST USES Ideal for small beds, edging borders or softening paths; suitable for city, rock and cottage gardens; does well in hanging baskets and pots

FLOWERS June to August

SCENTED No

ASPECT South or west facing, in a sheltered or exposed position; full sun

SOIL Any well-drained soil; dislikes sitting in winter wet

HARDINESS Frost hardy at temperatures down to -5°C/23°F; needs winter protection

DROUGHT TOLERANCE Good, once established

PROBLEMS None

CARE Trim lightly after flowering

PROPAGATION Division in spring; separate rooted runners from main plant and replant in spring, or pot up to grow larger and plant out later

Coreopsis verticillata 'Zagreb' 🎖 Tickseed

⬆ 30cm/12in ⬌ 30cm/12in   **EASY**

Born in the USA, tickseed is a bushy herbaceous perennial, usually found in woodland and open prairies. This reliably flowering, compact example has ferny, toothed, deep green leaves on numerous robust, thready stems, each topped with simple daisy-like sun yellow flowers, with the pointed petals radiating out from toast-brown centres. Tickseed usually has yellow flowers, but if you loathe yellows (and it's surprising how many gardeners do), opt for the lively *C.* 'Limerock Ruby' (50cm/20in) with deep red flowers or *C. rosea* 'American Dream' (45cm/18in) with small, pink, yellow-centred flowers.

BEST USES Ideal for bringing colour into the late-summer border; edging paths and planting at the front of borders; combines especially well with ornamental grasses; good for the wildlife garden as pollinating insects love it

FLOWERS July to September

SCENTED No

ASPECT Any, in a sheltered or exposed position; full sun to partial shade

SOIL Any fertile, well-drained soil

HARDINESS Fully hardy at temperatures down to -15°C/5°F; needs no winter protection

DROUGHT TOLERANCE Excellent, once established

PROBLEMS Slugs and snails

CARE Mulch with organic matter annually in spring

PROPAGATION Division in spring

Dianthus 'Becky Robinson' ♔
Pink

⬆ 25–45cm/10–18in ⬌ 40cm/16in   **EASY**

Pinks are evergreen, clump-forming perennials, native to Europe and Asia, that are ideal for smaller gardens. All have narrow, linear leaves which are usually blue/grey-green and form neat clumps. This modern cultivar with typical green-grey leaves makes compact hummocks from which arise dainty, slim, green stems, each topped with deliciously fragrant, clove-scented, lacy, double soft pink flowers, rimmed with vivid magenta with matching centres. *D.* 'Mrs Sinkins' has double creamy white flowers; *D.* 'Haytor Rock' ♔ has double, streaky pink and scarlet flowers; *D.* 'Doris' ♔ has semi-double soft pink flowers with raspberry centres.

> **BEST USES** Ideal for edging the border or along a path in the cottage garden; happy in containers; does well in gravel gardens and coastal conditions

FLOWERS June to August
SCENTED Yes
ASPECT South, east or west facing, in a sheltered or exposed position; full sun
SOIL Any fertile, moist, well-drained soil
HARDINESS Fully hardy at temperatures down to -15°C/5°F; needs no winter protection
DROUGHT TOLERANCE Good, once established
PROBLEMS Aphids, slugs and snails; rust
CARE Deadhead regularly to encourage further flowering; remove dead flower stems in autumn
PROPAGATION Cuttings (known as 'pipings') from non-flowering shoots in summer

Eryngium bourgatii Graham Stuart Thomas Sea holly

⬆ 55cm/22in ⬌ 30cm/12in   **EASY**

This clump-forming, tap-rooted herbaceous perennial from Spain is a dramatic, architectural plant, with deeply jagged, silver blue leaves with white striping, giving rise to stiff, blue-hued branched stems bearing thistle-like spiky flowers of metallic silver blue. Eryngiums like good drainage, but this variety will tolerate heavier soils than most. *E.b.* 'Oxford Blue' ♔ has dark silvery blue flowers with noticeable white veins.

> **BEST USES** A very structural plant, excellent for seaside gardens and in a gravel or Mediterranean garden; good for flower arrangers

FLOWERS June to August
SCENTED No
ASPECT South, east or west facing, in a sheltered or exposed position; full sun
SOIL Any fertile, well-drained soil; dislikes sitting in winter wet
HARDINESS Fully hardy at temperatures down to -15°C/5°F; needs no winter protection
DROUGHT TOLERANCE Excellent, once established
PROBLEMS Eelworms
CARE Cut back spent flower stems
PROPAGATION Sow ripe seed immediately in pots in a cold frame; root cuttings in late winter

HARDY GERANIUMS
Cranesbill

Geranium (Cinereum Group) 'Ballerina' ♈

↑ 15cm/6in ↔ 30cm/12in   **EASY**

Free-flowering hardy geraniums are a treasure trove of practicality, versatility and colour, but are not to be confused with pelargoniums, which are often referred to as geraniums: pelargoniums are lovely in their own right but are an altogether different proposition.

Hardy geraniums are herbaceous perennials that come from a wide variety of habitats across temperate regions of the world. They are undemanding and, with more than 300 species to choose from, there is one for most conditions, from dry and damp shade to hot sunny beds or banks. Any reasonably fertile soil will suit them, but they do not tolerate very wet conditions.

Some geraniums are annuals or biennials, but it is the hardy perennials that are the real workhorses in the border, flowering for long periods from spring through the summer with little or no maintenance and indispensable as very effective flowering ground cover; the lobed leaves may be scented or even evergreen. They range from compact (15cm/6in) to larger clump-forming varieties (up to 1.2m/4ft).

Most have simple cupped, shallow flowers (though some have reflexed or starry flowers) and come in graduating shades of blue, mauve, purple, magenta, pink and white. Those that flower in spring and early summer, such as G. 'Johnson's Blue' ♈, will often throw out a second show of flowers in late summer if the first flush is cut back after flowering.

No border should be without one variety.

The hardy geraniums deliver so much happiness for so little input, and this dwarf, clump-forming, spreading herbaceous perennial has much to recommend it, with evergreen, lobed, grey-green leaves and slender green stems, each bearing simple, saucer-shaped, purple-pink flowers, with deep purple veining on the petals. It flowers over a reasonable period in early summer, making it invaluable in smaller borders.

> **BEST USES** Ideal for almost any garden, from a city garden with small beds to a large country garden that needs low planting at the front of a border; excellent as ground cover for clothing awkward slopes and banks

FLOWERS May to July
SCENTED No
ASPECT South or west facing, in a sheltered position; full sun
SOIL Any fertile, well-drained soil
HARDINESS Fully hardy at temperatures down to -15°C/5°F; needs no winter protection
DROUGHT TOLERANCE Good, in short bursts, once established
PROBLEMS *Botrytis* (grey mould)
CARE Cut back faded flowers and tatty leaves as required; cut back hard in spring
PROPAGATION Division in spring

Geranium 'Jolly Bee' ♗

⬆ 60cm/24in ↔ 60cm/24in **EASY**

I've said it before and I'll say it again: the hardy geraniums are invaluable herbaceous perennials that grow generously and need little attention. This lovely new hybrid has felty, lobed, marbled leaves of a very fresh green and is smothered in simple, cupped, lavender blue flowers with white eyes and sooty stamens; the petals have attractive plum veining. Flowering prolifically from late spring to mid-autumn, it is one of the freest-flowering geraniums. G. Rozanne ♗ (*see opposite*) has violet blue flowers with white centres.

BEST USES Ideal ground cover as it spreads rapidly; grows well in containers; perfect in wildflower and cottage gardens or a formal border

FLOWERS May to October

SCENTED No

ASPECT Any, in a sheltered or exposed position; full sun to partial shade

SOIL Any fertile, well-drained soil; will not tolerate waterlogged soil

HARDINESS Fully hardy at temperatures down to -15°C/5°F; needs no winter protection

DROUGHT TOLERANCE Good, once established

PROBLEMS Slugs and snails; downy mildew in dry conditions

CARE Deadhead faded flower stems; remove tatty leaves after flowering; cut back hard in spring; mulch with organic matter annually in spring

PROPAGATION Division in spring; sow seed in situ or outdoors in pots, in spring or autumn

Geum 'Prinses Juliana'

⬆ 45cm/18in ↔ 75cm/30in **EASY**

Geums come from far and wide (Asia, Africa, Europe and South America) and most are rhizomatous herbaceous perennials. This clump-forming hybrid has bristly, oval to heart-shaped deep green leaves on longer than average stems, topped with semi-double orange flowers with pincushioned yellow eyes. It is a plant of long-flowering great cheer. Other recommended varieties include G. 'Mrs J. Bradshaw' ♗ (scarlet flowers) and G. 'Lady Stratheden' ♗ (double golden flowers).

BEST USES Suits any informal or cottagey border; does well in containers in a sunny city courtyard or on a patio

FLOWERS May to September

SCENTED No

ASPECT South, east or west facing, in a sheltered or exposed position; full sun

SOIL Any fertile, moist, well-drained soil

HARDINESS Fully hardy at temperatures down to -15°C/5°F; needs no winter protection

DROUGHT TOLERANCE Poor

PROBLEMS Aphids and sawfly larvae

CARE Trim back faded flowering stems; mulch with organic matter annually in spring

PROPAGATION Division in autumn or spring

Gypsophila 'Rosenschleier' (syn. *G.* 'Rosy Veil')

↑ 40–50cm/16–20in ⟷ 90cm/3ft   **EASY**

This semi-evergreen, spreading, mound-forming perennial (commonly known as Baby's breath) comes from arid stony areas of Europe and Asia. It has small, linear grey-green leaves that are almost completely camouflaged in summer by slender, wiry stems bearing frothy, dense clouds of abundant, tiny, dainty sprays of double white flowers that age to pink. This variety tolerates moist soil better than most. Other reliable species are *G. paniculata* 'Compacta Plena' (45cm/18in), with double white-pink flowers, and the much taller *G.p.* 'Bristol Fairy' (1.5m/5ft), with white flowers.

> **BEST USES** Lovely as a burst of diaphanous white or pink in an informal or cottage garden; excellent for clothing the bare lower limbs of leggy shrubs such as roses; a favourite with flower arrangers

FLOWERS June to September
SCENTED No
ASPECT South, east or west facing, in a sheltered position; full sun
SOIL Any fertile, light, well-drained soil; dislikes winter wet
HARDINESS Frost hardy at temperatures down to -5°C/23°F; needs winter protection
DROUGHT TOLERANCE Good, once established
PROBLEMS Stem rot
CARE Cut back the flowered stems to encourage a second moderate flowering; resents disturbance
PROPAGATION Root cuttings in late winter

Heuchera 'Persian Carpet'
Coral flower

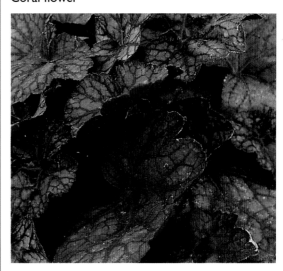

↑ 55–60cm/22–24in ⟷ 45–60cm/18–24in   **EASY**

Heucheras, largely from North America, are clump-forming evergreen or semi-evergreen perennials, valued for their foliage, which varies from greens to deep purples. This variety has especially handsome, deep plum-coloured, deeply lobed evergreen leaves, ghosted silver, which are gorgeous in spring. Tall, slender stems carry numerous, tiny, dainty creamy buff flowers in summer. *H.* 'Obsidian' is an absolute corker with even darker purple leaves; *H.* Crème Brûlée has apricot-amber leaves.

> **BEST USES** Great ground cover in the cottage garden and spring border, planted en masse; excellent for containers; can be grown in a raised bed or rock garden

FLOWERS May
SCENTED No
ASPECT South, east or west facing, in a sheltered or exposed position; full sun to partial shade
SOIL Any fertile, moist, well-drained soil
HARDINESS Fully hardy at temperatures down to -15°C/5°F; needs no winter protection
DROUGHT TOLERANCE Poor
PROBLEMS None; leaves fade in full shade
CARE Remove faded flower stems after flowering
PROPAGATION Division in autumn

....

GREENFINGER TIP *Frosts are notorious for heaving heucheras from the soil: when this happens, firm them back down well*

Hosta 'Fire and Ice'
Plantain lily

⬆ 60cm/24in ⬌ 90cm/3ft   **EASY**

Hostas are clump-forming herbaceous perennials, originally from Asia, with countless hybrids from the USA. The striking, sculptural foliage comes in all sizes and can be pleated, corrugated, heavily veined, puckered, glossy or matt, in many shades of green, sometimes with cream or gold margins or splashes. This compact variety has large, puckered, heart-shaped leaves that are a rich deep green, splashed with creamy-white centres, and smooth, upright stems that bear funnel-shaped lavender flowers through summer. *H.* 'Golden Tiara' ⚘ (35cm/14in) has rounded lime green leaves with pea green centres; *H.* 'Hadspen Blue' (Tardiana Group) (25cm/10in) has quilted grey-green leaves; both have lavender flowers.

BEST USES Particularly useful in a shady garden, adding sculptural leaf shape to a formal or modern planting scheme; looks very smart planted in containers in a chic city garden or roof terrace

FLOWERS July to August; grown for foliage
SCENTED No
ASPECT North, east or west facing, in a sheltered position; partial shade
SOIL Any fertile, moist, well-drained soil; dislikes chalk
HARDINESS Fully hardy at temperatures down to -15°C/5°F; needs no winter protection
DROUGHT TOLERANCE Poor
PROBLEMS Slugs, snails and vine weevil
CARE Mulch with organic matter annually in spring
PROPAGATION Division after flowering in summer

Incarvillea delavayi
Hardy gloxinia

⬆ 60cm/24in ⬌ 30cm/12in   **EASY**

This clump-forming herbaceous perennial, of Asian origin, has deeply divided fern-like green leaves, and produces frilled, trumpet-shaped flowers of deep rose, with yellow throats, on short, sturdy stems from early to mid-summer. It has a long taproot, which no doubt aids its drought resistance, and interesting, plump, green pointed seed pods. *I.d.* 'Snowtop' has white funnelled flowers; *I.d.* 'Bees' Pink' has light pink flowers. I have a confession to make – much as I've tried to like them over the years, to my eye, their proportions are all wrong.

BEST USES Excellent for vivid colour in a raised spring border, traditional or cottage garden; does well in pots in a sunny courtyard garden

FLOWERS May to June
SCENTED No
ASPECT South, east or west facing, in a sheltered position; full sun to partial shade
SOIL Any fertile, moist, well-drained soil
HARDINESS Fully hardy/borderline at temperatures down to -15°C/5°F; may need winter protection in colder areas
DROUGHT TOLERANCE Good, once established
PROBLEMS Slugs and snails
CARE Mulch with organic matter annually in spring; deadhead fading flowers; protect crowns from frost
PROPAGATION Sow seed in pots in a cold frame in spring or autumn (autumn-sown seedlings will need frost protection)

Lamium maculatum 'Beacon Silver'
Deadnettle

↑ 20cm/8in ⬌ 90cm/3ft   **EASY**

Lamium is a low-growing, rhizomatous, semi-evergreen herbaceous perennial from Europe and Asia that makes excellent ground cover. This striking variety has nettle-like silver leaves, edged with green, and produces a profusion of spiked, whorled magenta pink flowers on short green stems. Lamium is a plant for all seasons and, given plenty of organic matter when planting and a generous annual top-up, it can survive drought well. Others recommended are the lovely white-flowered *L.m.* 'White Nancy' ♛ , and *L.m.* 'Pink Pearls', with white-splashed leaves and mid-pink flowers.

> **BEST USES** Perfect for the woodland or cottage garden or as ground cover in a shrubbery and on gentle slopes where the lawnmower won't reach

FLOWERS May to July
SCENTED No
ASPECT North, east or west facing, in a sheltered position; partial to full shade
SOIL Any fertile, humus-rich, moist, well-drained soil; add organic matter before planting
HARDINESS Fully hardy at temperatures down to -15°C/5°F; needs no winter protection
DROUGHT TOLERANCE Good, once established
PROBLEMS Slugs and snails
CARE Trim back after flowering to encourage new growth; mulch with organic matter annually in spring
PROPAGATION Division in early spring or autumn

Liatris spicata 'Kobold'
Gayfeather/Blazing star

↑ 60cm/24in ⬌ 45cm/18in   **EASY**

Liatris is an upright tuberous perennial from the USA, with narrow, flat, pointed basal leaves. It forms neat clumps with stiff, upright, smooth stems, topped with erect, fluffy, bottlebrush-like flower spikes of deep pink that open successively from the top downwards, in late summer. *L.s.* 'Alba' has white flowers; the slightly taller *L.s.* 'Floristan Violett' (75cm/30in) has dense violet flowers. They thrive in moist soil, but are reasonably drought tolerant if organic matter is added when planting.

> **BEST USES** A dependable plant for adding vertical accents in the front of the border; also good for the wildflower or prairie garden

FLOWERS August to September
SCENTED No
ASPECT South or west facing, in a sheltered or exposed position; full sun
SOIL Any fertile, well-drained soil
HARDINESS Fully hardy at temperatures down to -15°C/5°F; needs no winter protection
DROUGHT TOLERANCE Medium, once established
PROBLEMS Mice, slugs and snails nibble roots
CARE May need staking in windy areas
PROPAGATION Division in spring; sow seed in pots in a cold frame in autumn

Nepeta × *faassenii* ♗
Catmint

⬆ 45cm/18in ⬅➡ 45cm/18in · · · · · · · · · · EASY

A bushy, clump-forming perennial of garden origin that is loved by gardeners and cats alike. This compact variety has aromatic, rounded, wrinkled sage green leaves, arranged along soft, spreading stems. The flowering spikes open to masses of small, lavender blue flowers that last and last over the summer. When crushed (or when your cats flatten it, which they inevitably will), the foliage releases a herbal, minty scent.

BEST USES Good at the front of a border or edging paths in an informal garden; a great choice for the gravel and Mediterranean garden

FLOWERS June to September
SCENTED Aromatic leaves
ASPECT South, east or west facing, in a sheltered or exposed position; full sun to partial shade
SOIL Any fertile, well-drained soil
HARDINESS Fully hardy at temperatures down to -15°C/5°F; needs no winter protection
DROUGHT TOLERANCE Excellent, once established
PROBLEMS Slugs and snails nibble young foliage; powdery mildew
CARE Cut back after flowering to prevent it becoming straggly and for a modest second flush of flowers; insert bamboo canes to prevent the cats lying in the middle of it
PROPAGATION Division in autumn or spring

Oenothera fruticosa 'Fyrverkeri' (syn. *O.f.* Fireworks) ♗ Evening primrose

⬆ 30cm/12in ⬅➡ 30cm/12in · · · · · · · · · · EASY

This erect, short-lived herbaceous perennial or biennial from North America produces lance-shaped branching leaves, tinted bronze-brown, with long, strong, reddish leafy stems studded with red buds that open to reveal large, sweetly fragrant, bowl-shaped bright yellow flowers. These open in the early evening and fade by sunrise the next day, superseded by yet more one-day-wonder blooms. Other notable varieties include *O.f.* 'African Sun' (clear yellow flowers) and *O.f.* 'Yellow River' (golden flowers); both are taller, at 60cm/24in.

BEST USES Ideal for cottage gardens and formal borders; does well in containers or pots and looks equally pleasing in a wildflower garden

FLOWERS June to August
SCENTED Scented flowers
ASPECT South or west facing, in a sheltered position; full sun
SOIL Any poor to fertile, well-drained soil
HARDINESS Fully hardy at temperatures down to -15°C/5°F; needs no winter protection
DROUGHT TOLERANCE Good, once established
PROBLEMS Slugs and snails; powdery mildew
CARE Cut back spent flower stems after flowering
PROPAGATION Self-seeds easily once established; sow seed in pots in a cold frame in spring

Papaver nudicaule Gartenzwerg Group ♉ (formerly *P.n.* Garden Gnome Group)

⬆ 30cm/12in ⬌ 30cm/12in   **EASY**

Oh, the jewel-coloured flowers of poppies make me happy! They are traditional cottage garden favourites, from small, simple-flowered annual poppies to the more extravagant, tall herbaceous types, coming in every hue under the sun. This ever-so-common, short-lived, bushy herbaceous perennial (commonly known as Iceland poppy) lacks the showiness of its Oriental cousins, but is uncomplicated and joyful. It has finely dissected, bristly light green leaves that form a basal clump, from which arise wiry stems, each topped with a simple, shallow bowl-shaped tissue-papery flower, in salmon pink to orange and yellow. Each bloom has yellow eyelash stamens and no two flowers ever seem to be the same shade. Bliss.

BEST USES A must for the cottage garden; thrives happily studded at the front of beds and borders

FLOWERS May to July
SCENTED No
ASPECT South or west facing, in a sheltered or exposed position; full sun
SOIL Any well-drained soil, especially light or loamy soil
HARDINESS Fully hardy at temperatures down to -15°C/5°F; needs no winter protection
DROUGHT TOLERANCE Excellent, once established
PROBLEMS Aphids; downy mildew
CARE None
PROPAGATION Division in autumn or early spring; sow seed in situ in spring

Persicaria affinis 'Darjeeling Red' ♉
Bistort/Knotweed

⬆ 20cm/8in ⬌ 30cm/12in   **EASY**

There are many species of persicaria, coming from a wide variety of habitats the world over. This one is a mat-forming, evergreen perennial from the Himalayas and has bright green lance-shaped leaves. Pink, slender, upright stems arise from the bed of foliage, topped with tiny cupped flowers, tightly clustered to form pink flower spikes that turn a warm red as they mature from mid-summer to autumn. *P.a.* 'Donald Lowndes' ♉ has pale pink flowers.

BEST USES An elegant addition at the front of a shady border or in a woodland garden or informal planting scheme; makes excellent ground cover on awkward slopes; outstanding for the wildflower garden, as insects love it

FLOWERS June to September
SCENTED No
ASPECT South, east or west facing, in a sheltered or exposed position; full sun to partial shade
SOIL Any fertile, humus-rich, moist, well-drained soil
HARDINESS Fully hardy at temperatures down to -15°C/5°F; needs no winter protection
DROUGHT TOLERANCE Poor
PROBLEMS None; plants can be invasive
CARE Mulch with organic matter annually in spring; remove dead flower stems after flowering
PROPAGATION Division in autumn or spring; sow seed in pots in a cold frame in spring

Phuopsis stylosa 'Purpurea'
Caucasian crosswort

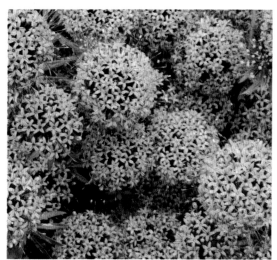

↑ 20cm/8in ↔ 50cm/20in   **EASY**

This Caucasian, semi-evergreen, mat-forming herbaceous perennial is ideal for the beginner because it is both low maintenance and problem free. It makes a dense carpet of whorls of aromatic (slightly musky), narrow, linear mid-green leaves, sparsely arranged on short, slender green stems, topped with purple-pink drumstick heads, made up of tiny, sweetly scented tubular flowers, from mid-summer to early autumn. This is the only variety worth mentioning.

BEST USES Ideal for making ground cover in a rock garden, or as an edging plant at the front of the border; it is also happy left to straddle a wall or slope or grown in a container on a city patio

FLOWERS July to September
SCENTED Aromatic leaves and scented flowers
ASPECT Any, in a sheltered or exposed position; full sun to partial shade
SOIL Any fertile, moist, well-drained soil
HARDINESS Fully hardy at temperatures down to -15°C/5°F; needs no winter protection
DROUGHT TOLERANCE Excellent, once established
PROBLEMS None
CARE Cut back after flowering to encourage dense foliage
PROPAGATION Division in spring to early summer; sow seed in pots in a cold frame in autumn

Platycodon grandiflorus ♉
Balloon flower

↑ 60cm/24in ↔ 30cm/12in   **EASY**

Originally from Japan, this tidy, compact, clump-forming herbaceous perennial has narrow, lance-shaped leaves that are bluish to mid-green, arranged in sparse whorls around upright stems. Clusters of single purple-blue flower buds are initially shaped like small inflated balloons but open to reveal simple, campanula-like, star-shaped, cupped, five-petalled flowers (5cm/2in across), with pronounced darker veining. *P.g.* 'Park's Double Blue' has darker, violet blue flowers; *P.g.* 'Albus' has white ballooned flowers.

BEST USES A charming addition to the front of borders; does well in containers; enjoys free-draining soil, so try this in a gravel garden

FLOWERS July to August
SCENTED No
ASPECT South, east or west facing, in a sheltered or exposed position; full sun to partial shade
SOIL Any fertile, moist, well-drained soil
HARDINESS Fully hardy at temperatures down to -15°C/5°F; needs no winter protection
DROUGHT TOLERANCE Poor
PROBLEMS Slugs and snails nibble young leaves
CARE May need staking; mulch with organic matter annully in spring; remove spent flower heads and cut down to the base in autumn
PROPAGATION Division in summer; sow seed in situ in spring

Polemonium 'Lambrook Mauve' ♀
Jacob's ladder

⬆ 45cm/18in ⬌ 45cm/18in   **EASY**

A friend said, 'You can't be without this in the book – it's gorgeous!' I can't help but agree. This European clump-forming herbaceous perennial gets its name from the pointed, fresh green leaves, arranged on upright stems like ladder steps, which emerge from low, leafy basal growth. It produces clusters of bell-shaped, five-petalled lilac-blue flowers with yellow centres and stamens, in late spring to summer: it's not often you find something that flowers so profusely in semi-shade. It can be short-lived, but it self-seeds with great ease.

BEST USES Enhances any flower border, whether formal or cottagey; also good in lightly dappled woodland or the wildflower garden

FLOWERS May to June
SCENTED No
ASPECT South, east or west facing, in a sheltered or exposed position; full sun to partial shade
SOIL Any fertile, moist, well-drained soil
HARDINESS Fully hardy at temperatures down to -15°C/5°F; needs no winter protection
DROUGHT TOLERANCE Poor
PROBLEMS Powdery mildew
CARE Deadhead after flowering; mulch with organic matter annually in spring
PROPAGATION Self-seeds easily; division in spring

Primula vialii ♀
Vial's primrose

⬆ 60cm/24in ⬌ 30cm/12in   **EASY**

This exceptional, if short-lived, orchid-type primrose from Asia is perfect for borders and damp spots. It is a hardy herbaceous perennial with long, oblong fresh green leaves forming a rosette-like basal clump, but it's the flowers that steal the show. Tall, strong, smooth, straight bright green stems each bear a single, elegant flowering spike, comprising masses of tiny, star-shaped pale lilac flowers at the base, graduating to bright brick red at the tips of the flowering spires. This variety doesn't self-seed as well as one would like, which is a shame for such a lovely plant.

BEST USES Ideal for the cottage garden; excellent for shady, damp borders or planted by a pond

FLOWERS June to July
SCENTED No
ASPECT North, east or west facing, in a sheltered or exposed position; partial shade
SOIL Any fertile, moist, well-drained soil
HARDINESS Fully hardy at temperatures down to -15°C/5°F; needs no winter protection
DROUGHT TOLERANCE Poor
PROBLEMS Aphids, slugs, snails and vine weevil; *Botrytis* (grey mould)
CARE Mulch with organic matter annually in spring
PROPAGATION Division in late autumn or early spring

Sanguisorba 'Tanna'
Burnet

↑ 30cm/12in ↔ 40cm/16in **EASY**

Sanguisorba is a great favourite of mine. A clump-forming herbaceous perennial of Japanese origin, it has aromatic, rounded, blue-green leaves with slightly wavy edges (they are edible and can be used in salads). Masses of short, wire-thin, branching stems, topped with oval drumsticks of rich, deep maroon red, are sent up in exuberant abundance.

BEST USES Ideal for the cottage garden; perfect in a prairie planting scheme; excellent for extending livid colour into the autumn in flower beds; bees and butterflies adore it, so a very good choice for the wildlife garden

FLOWERS June to September
SCENTED Aromatic leaves
ASPECT South, east or west facing, in a sheltered or exposed position; full sun to partial shade
SOIL Any fertile, well-drained soil
HARDINESS Fully hardy at temperatures down to -15°C/5°F; needs no winter protection
DROUGHT TOLERANCE Poor
PROBLEMS Slugs and snails nibble young foliage
CARE Deadhead to prevent self-seeding; may become invasive
PROPAGATION Division in autumn or spring; sow seed in pots in a cold frame in autumn or spring

Sedum spathulifolium 'Cape Blanco' ♛

↑ 60cm/24in ↔ 30cm/12in **EASY**

Sedums are very useful plants in parched borders, where they bring interesting colour and form to the garden. They are invariably succulent-leaved and the flowers, which are mainly star-shaped, range through pink, white, yellow and purple. In height they vary from the diminutive (5cm/2in) to taller border plants (60cm/24in). This North American offering is one of the small mat-forming evergreen perennials, with tiny, fleshy, rounded silver leaves, often flushed bronze, and short, brittle stems, bearing masses of small, flat-headed, star-shaped bright yellow flowers. S.s. 'Purpureum' ♛ has silver and plum-flushed leaves and yellow flowers, and is much the same size.

BEST USES Excellent for hot, dry, borders; looks very much at home in Mediterranean or gravel gardens

FLOWERS June to July
SCENTED No
ASPECT South or west facing, in a sheltered or exposed position; full sun
SOIL Any well-drained soil
HARDINESS Fully hardy at temperatures down to -15°C/5°F; needs no winter protection
DROUGHT TOLERANCE Excellent, once established
PROBLEMS Slugs and snails; fungal diseases
CARE None
PROPAGATION Division in late autumn

Stachys byzantina
Lamb's ears

↑ 45cm/18in ↔ 60cm/24in   **EASY**

Originating from Turkey and Iran, this upright, mat-forming evergreen perennial is quite enchanting and always a great curiosity with children. It has tactile rosettes of velvety grey leaves that are densely covered in soft white wool. Stiff spikes of purple flowers are borne in summer, through to early autumn in long, hot summers. The soft leaves really do feel like a bunny's or lamb's ears, so this is great for encouraging children's interest in plants.
S.b. 'Silver Carpet' is a non-flowering variety; *S.b.* 'Big Ears' has felty, mid-green leaves that are longer than average (25cm/10in).

BEST USES Ideal for ground cover in a hot sunny border, on a gently sloping bank or in a Mediterranean or gravel garden; also pretty in a cottage garden; attractive to pollinating insects

FLOWERS June to September
SCENTED No
ASPECT South, east or west facing, in a sheltered or exposed position; full sun
SOIL Any fertile, well-drained soil
HARDINESS Fully hardy at temperatures down to -15°C/5°F; needs no winter protection
DROUGHT TOLERANCE Excellent, once established
PROBLEMS Powdery mildew
CARE Remove faded flower stems to prevent self-seeding
PROPAGATION Self-seeds easily; division in spring

Tricyrtis formosana 'Dark Beauty'
Toad lily

↑ 50cm/20in ↔ 30cm/12in   **MEDIUM**

Made in Taiwan, this exotic-looking upright rhizomatous perennial has smooth, polished, lance-shaped dark green leaves and maroon-brown branching stems, which carry the flowers well above the leaves, making a striking contrast. Bullet-shaped, deep plum buds open to reveal striking, curiously fleshy, six-petalled, star-shaped purple-spotted flowers (some 4cm/1½in across) with purple-mottled upright centres.

BEST USES A must for natural woodland areas and gloomy, north-facing shady borders; a useful addition to the pond or water's edge where it can keep its roots moist

FLOWERS August to September
SCENTED No
ASPECT North, east or west facing, in a sheltered or exposed position; partial to full shade
SOIL Any fertile, humus-rich, moisture-retentive soil
HARDINESS Fully hardy at temperatures down to -15°C/5°F; needs no winter protection
DROUGHT TOLERANCE Poor
PROBLEMS Slugs and snails in spring
CARE Dry mulch in winter in colder regions; dislikes disturbance
PROPAGATION Division in early spring; sow ripe seed immediately in pots in a cold frame

GREENFINGER TIP *When growing from seed in colder regions, overwinter plantlets in a greenhouse in the first year*

Tulbaghia violacea 'Alba'

⬆ 30cm/12in ⬌ 30cm/12in   **MEDIUM**

This clump-forming, frost-hardy, rhizomatous perennial comes from South Africa. It has narrow straps of grey-green foliage and sends up very straight, erect, smooth, leafless green stems topped with fragrant, tubular white flowers, with pale pink stamens, hiding in creamy funnels. The garlic-smelling pale mauve version, *T. violacea* (60cm/24in), is more vigorous than the white variety but marginally less hardy, so needs winter nursing; *T.v.* 'Silver Lace' (50cm/20in) has pale mauve flowers with light green variegated leaves.

BEST USES Plant in a sheltered, sunny border near the house to appreciate the sweet scent and profuse flowering; will grow in pots if kept well drained, well watered and well fed

FLOWERS July to September
SCENTED Scented flowers
ASPECT South or west facing, in a sheltered position, with protection from winds; full sun
SOIL Any fertile, humus-rich, well-drained soil
HARDINESS Frost hardy at temperatures down to -5°C/23°F; needs winter protection (hardier in well-drained soil, where it takes brief lows of -10°C/14°F)
DROUGHT TOLERANCE Good
PROBLEMS Aphids
CARE Mulch with organic matter annually in spring; remove faded flower stems; dry mulch in winter
PROPAGATION Division in spring every three years, otherwise flowering diminishes; sow ripe seed immediately in pots in a cold frame

Veronica austriaca subsp. teucrium 'Royal Blue' ♝

⬆ 30cm/12in ⬌ 30cm/12in   **EASY**

This mat-forming herbaceous perennial from Europe may be small, but what a beauty! Commonly known as Saw-leaved speedwell, it has lance-shaped, slightly toothed, bristly mid-green leaves that make restrained mounds, from which arise upright, slender flower spires, studded along their length with small, simple, shallow, cupped flowers of azure blue, with deep blue veins and greeny white eyes. *V.a.* subsp. *t.* 'Crater Lake Blue' ♝ is the same size with darker blue flowers.

BEST USES A lovely, elegant plant for the front of the border or edging pathways; perfect for the cottage garden; positively embraces coastal conditions

FLOWERS May to June
SCENTED No
ASPECT South, east or west facing, in a sheltered position; full sun to partial shade
SOIL Any moist, well-drained soil; dislikes winter wet
HARDINESS Fully hardy at temperatures down to -15°C/5°F; needs no winter protection
DROUGHT TOLERANCE Poor
PROBLEMS Downy and powdery mildew
CARE Remove faded spent flowers
PROPAGATION Division in autumn or spring

GREENFINGER TIP *Veronicas tend to get weak and unproductive: divide them every three years or so to keep them at their best*

Achillea 'Summerwine' ♀
Yarrow

⬆ 90cm/3ft ⬌ 50cm/20in   **EASY**

Yarrows are incredibly attractive upright, rhizomatous hardy perennials from temperate grasslands and originally consisted of largely yellow varieties. Nowadays, the range of colours includes buff, beige, apricot and some divine pinks and lilacs as well as golden yellow. This variety has muskily aromatic, filigreed, dark green leaves and tall straight stems, supporting flat flower heads of deep rosy red flowers with white centres in summer. Other recommended species are *A. millefolium* 'Red Beauty' (deep red) and *A.m.* 'Dark Lilac Beauty'.

BEST USES An architectural plant that combines well with grasses in prairie and gravel gardens; a must for wildflower gardens as it is loved by bees and butterflies; tolerant of coastal locations

FLOWERS July to August

SCENTED Aromatic leaves

ASPECT South, east or west facing, in a sheltered or exposed position; full sun

SOIL Any fertile, moist, well-drained soil

HARDINESS Fully hardy/borderline at temperatures down to -15°C/5°F; may need winter protection in colder areas

DROUGHT TOLERANCE Good, once established

PROBLEMS Aphids; powdery mildew

CARE May need staking as the flower heads can soak up rain like sponges and flop over; cut down to ground level in late autumn or early spring

PROPAGATION Division in spring

Alstroemeria 'Orange Glory' ♀
Peruvian lily

⬆ 90cm/3ft ⬌ 90cm/3ft   **EASY**

Alstroemerias are upright, tuberous perennials from the grasslands of South America that have a reputation for being a bit fickle: they have a short flowering season and can be difficult to establish. Typically, they have very slender, brittle, wand-like green stems that branch into multiple buds of delicate flared funnelled flowers, ranging in colour from yellow to salmon, red, pink and white. This one is easy and reliable once it has settled down and has stouter stems than most, with narrow, bright green leaves and exuberant, showy orange flowers, with speckled yellow throats. *A.* 'Phoenix' has deep wine-coloured flowers; *A.* 'Elvira' has creamy pink, white-striped flowers.

BEST USES Wonderful in containers and perfect for bringing exotic colour into the garden; does well in informal borders or mixed beds

FLOWERS June to August, often later

SCENTED No

ASPECT Any, in a sheltered or exposed position; full sun to partial shade

SOIL Any fertile, moist, well-drained soil

HARDINESS Fully hardy at temperatures down to -15°C/5°F; needs no winter protection

DROUGHT TOLERANCE Poor

PROBLEMS Caterpillars, slugs and snails

CARE Cut down spent flower stems, leaving tubers underground; dry mulch in winter in colder areas

PROPAGATION Division in spring

Anchusa azurea 'Loddon Royalist' 🎖
Alkanet

⬆ 90cm/3ft ⬌ 60cm/24in   **EASY**

This clump-forming herbaceous perennial from southern Europe has a sturdy, upright habit with narrow, rough, bristly lance-shaped dark green leaves. It is not the most attractive foliage plant, but the branching stems carrying a profusion of simple, small, tubular, star-shaped royal blue flowers (which must be one of the brightest blues about), making it a knockout for summer colour. Recommended varieties include *A.a.* 'Opal', with pale blue flowers, and the dwarf variety *A.a.* 'Little John' (45cm/18in × 30cm/12in), with blue flowers.

BEST USES Lovely for the cottage garden; perfect for wildlife gardens as insects love it; blends beautifully in a Mediterranean or gravel garden

FLOWERS June

SCENTED No

ASPECT Any, in a sheltered position; full sun

SOIL Any fertile, moist, well-drained soil; intolerant of wet winter soil

HARDINESS Fully hardy at temperatures down to -15°C/5°F; needs no winter protection

DROUGHT TOLERANCE Poor

PROBLEMS Powdery mildew

CARE Deadhead spent flower heads to prolong flowering; cut stems back to ground level in autumn

PROPAGATION Sow seed in pots in a cold frame in spring; root cuttings in winter

GREENFINGER TIP *Replace plants every five years; younger plants produce better flower displays*

Chelone glabra
Turtlehead

⬆ 90cm/3ft ⬌ 45cm/18in   **EASY**

These upright herbaceous perennials from North America are a bit of an oddity, but appealing none the less. The narrow, vein-etched, deep green leaves are sparsely arranged up very sturdy, squarish, erect stems and produce short spikes of white-hooded, pink-tinged flowers, which resemble a turtle head. They are slow growing but bring interest to shady areas and are invaluable in a damp or boggy garden. *C. obliqua* (pink flowers) and *C.o.* var. *alba* (white flowers) are similar, but more manageable at 60cm/24in tall.

BEST USES Excellent for a shady damp spot or a boggy area in the garden; adds interesting form at the side of a pond

FLOWERS July to September

SCENTED No

ASPECT Any, in a sheltered or exposed position; full sun to partial shade

SOIL Any fertile, deep, moist soil; ideal for heavy clay and boggy or wet ground

HARDINESS Fully hardy at temperatures down to -15°C/5°F; needs no winter protection

DROUGHT TOLERANCE Poor

PROBLEMS Slugs and snails

CARE Mulch well with organic matter annually in mid-spring

PROPAGATION Division in spring; sow seed in pots in a cold frame in spring

Dictamnus albus var. purpureus ☿
Burning bush/Purple flowered dittany

⬆ 90cm/3ft ⬌ 60cm/24in　　　　**EASY**

This woody-based clump-forming perennial, from Asia and southern Europe, is a low-maintenance plant with distinctive, pinnate, lemon-scented leaves and bears pretty, scented flower spikes made up of individual, small, star-shaped, veined rosy purple flowers in late spring to mid-summer. The flowers and seeds contain flammable oils, hence the common name. *D. albus* is more compact (from 40cm/16in tall), with white flowers.

> **BEST USES** Ideal in hot, sunny borders or the cottage garden; combines well with most traditional herbaceous or Mediterranean grey foliage plants

FLOWERS May to July
SCENTED Lemon-scented foliage; scented flowers
ASPECT Any, in a sheltered or exposed position; full sun to partial shade
SOIL Any fertile, well-drained soil
HARDINESS Fully hardy at temperatures down to -15°C/5°F; needs no winter protection
DROUGHT TOLERANCE Excellent, once established
PROBLEMS None
CARE Foliage dies back in winter; or cut back to ground level in autumn
PROPAGATION Division in autumn or spring; sow ripe seed immediately in pots in a cold frame

....

GREENFINGER TIP *This resents being moved and will sulk for a season: give a good organic mulch at the base of the plant to help the roots re-establish*

Digitalis × mertonensis ☿
Foxglove

⬆ 90cm/3ft ⬌ 30cm/12in　　　　**EASY**

Foxgloves are cottage garden favourites, and most are clump-forming biennials, but this lovely hybrid is a hardy perennial. It has bristly, lance-shaped, toothy, wrinkled deep green leaves with pronounced veining, and bears elegant, upright, flowering spires, studded with faded, dusky pink deep-throated flowers, speckled with pale brown nectar guides. *D. purpurea* f. *albiflora* (syn. *D.p.* 'Alba') ☿ (1.2m/4ft) has white flowers; *D.* 'Glory of Roundway' (80cm/32in) has smaller, pale apricot-pink flowers with maroon spotting.

> **BEST USES** Plant in drifts through the middle of the border for vertical accents with a natural effect; wonderful for shady woodland planting; will colonise over the years, being well-loved by pollinating bees

FLOWERS May to June
SCENTED No
ASPECT Any, in a sheltered or exposed position; full sun to partial shade
SOIL Any humus-rich, moist, fertile, well-drained soil except waterlogged; add organic matter when planting
HARDINESS Fully hardy at temperatures down to -15°C/5°F; needs no winter protection
DROUGHT TOLERANCE Good, once established
PROBLEMS Powdery mildew
CARE Cut down dead flower spikes to limit self-seeding, or leave seed to ripen and scatter
PROPAGATION Self-seeds easily; surface sow seed in pots in a cold frame in spring; this hybrid comes true from seed if not planted near other varieties

Echinacea purpurea 'Robert Bloom'
Coneflower

⬆ 90cm/3ft ↔ 60cm/24in   **EASY**

The North American coneflowers are stiffly upright, deep-rooting herbaceous perennials with coarse, lance-shaped deep green leaves on tall, sturdy, self-supporting stems, topped with large, single, daisy-like flowers, with prominent central cones. They are usually pink or white, but there are some corking new yellow and orange varieties. This flamboyant, fragrant variety has slightly drooping, rich cerise flowers (10cm/4in across) and tactile orange-brown cones. *E.p.* 'Kim's Knee High' (50cm/20in) has deep rosy pink flowers; *E.p.* 'White Lustre' (75cm/30in) has white flowers.

BEST USES Magnificent planted with ornamental grasses in a contemporary garden or formal border, or a prairie planting scheme; irresistible to bees

FLOWERS June to September

SCENTED Yes

ASPECT South, east or west facing, in a sheltered or exposed position; full sun to partial shade; flowering is reduced in shade

SOIL Any fertile, moist, humus-rich, well-drained soil

HARDINESS Fully hardy at temperatures down to -15°C/5°F; needs no winter protection

DROUGHT TOLERANCE Good, once established

PROBLEMS None

CARE Needs no staking; cut back spent flowers for a modest second flowering; cut back to ground level in autumn; resents disturbance

PROPAGATION Division in autumn or spring

Echinops ritro 'Veitch's Blue' ♉
Globe thistle

⬆ 90cm/3ft ↔ 45cm/18in   **EASY**

Echinops are architectural plants, with prickly leaves and thistle-like, domed flower heads. This upright, clump-forming herbaceous perennial from dry, rocky places in Europe is very vigorous, with prickly, jagged grey-green leaves, stiffly upright branching stems and shimmering deep blue flowers, reminiscent of thistled drumsticks, that last well into winter as seed heads. All are tolerant of drought and poor soils, and there are none I dislike, so spoil yourself and grow several: *E. sphaerocephalus* 'Arctic Glow' (1.5m/5ft) has ghostly white domed flower heads; *E. bannaticus* (1.2m/4ft) has grey-blue leaves and globed, powder blue flowers.

BEST USES Ideal as a focal point in a gravel or Mediterranean garden; attracts hordes of bees and butterflies; appeals equally to dried flower arrangers

FLOWERS June to August

SCENTED No

ASPECT South, east or west facing, in a sheltered or exposed position; full sun to partial shade

SOIL Any well-drained soil; may be short-lived on clay

HARDINESS Fully hardy at temperatures down to -15°C/5°F; needs no winter protection

DROUGHT TOLERANCE Excellent, once established

PROBLEMS Aphids

CARE Deadhead to prevent self-seeding or leave faded flower spikes for late-season interest

PROPAGATION Division in autumn to spring; root cuttings in winter

Euphorbia griffithii 'Dixter' 🎖
Spurge

⬆ 75cm/30in ⬌ 90cm/3ft   **EASY**

This deciduous, rhizomatous herbaceous perennial is a really punchy colour and provides a reasonable period of interest. It has attractive, lance-shaped dark green leaves, edged in salmon, and distinctive pink central leaf veins. But it is the fiery, burnt orange of the flower bracts, held on straight, deep red stems, that makes it so appealing. A must-have. *E. griffithii* 'Fireglow' has deep green leaves with red central ribs and rich orange flower heads from summer to autumn.

> **BEST USES** Great for chic city gardens and the cottage garden alike; tolerant of some shade so can cope with woodland gardens or north-facing borders

FLOWERS June to September

SCENTED No

ASPECT Any, in a sheltered or exposed position; full sun to partial shade (but the colour is best in full sun)

SOIL Any fertile, moist, well-drained soil

HARDINESS Fully hardy at temperatures down to -15°C/5°F; needs no winter protection

DROUGHT TOLERANCE Poor

PROBLEMS None

CARE Cut back spent flower stems in autumn

PROPAGATION Division in spring; sow seed in pots in a cold frame in spring

Francoa sonchifolia
Maiden's wreath

⬆ 75cm/30in ⬌ 45cm/18in   **EASY**

This South American native is often seen in cottage gardens, but should be used more widely as it is easy to grow, downright determined to give of its best and pretty much trouble free. It is a clump-forming hardy herbaceous perennial with broad, deeply lobed, hairy, dark green leaves in rosette formation at the base. Tall, thin, upright, slender green wands, flushed pink, are studded with pretty spires of shallow, simple four-petalled, pinky white flowers, each petal with a deep rose pink marking.

> **BEST USES** An informal plant for the cottage garden; ideal for the wildflower garden, attracting its fair share of pollinating insects

FLOWERS July to August

SCENTED No

ASPECT South, east or west facing, in a sheltered or exposed position; full sun to partial shade

SOIL Any fertile, humus-rich, moist, well-drained soil

HARDINESS Frost hardy at temperatures down to -5°C/23°F; needs winter protection

DROUGHT TOLERANCE Poor

PROBLEMS None

CARE May need staking; deadhead spent flowers to encourage a second flowering; cut back leaves in spring

PROPAGATION Division in spring

Gentiana asclepiadea 🏅
Willow gentian

⬆ 90cm/3ft ↔ 45cm/18in   **MEDIUM**

Gentians are well known as small carpeting alpines, but can also be large herbaceous plants. This tall European clump-forming herbaceous perennial has pointed, willow-like mid-green leaves arranged in opposite pairs up straight stems. These arch as the plants mature and bear twinned tubular trumpets of rich blue flowers (4cm/1½in long) from late summer to early autumn. It can be fussy about soil, but will thrive in the right conditions. *G.a.* 'Alba' (50cm/20in) has pure white flowers; *G.a.* 'Knightshayes' (50cm/20in) has bright blue, white-throated flowers; *G.a.* 'Pink Swallow' (40cm/16in) has pale pink trumpets with brown spotting.

BEST USES An old reliable in the cottage garden or informal border; excellent in a woodland garden; does well in a north-facing flower border

FLOWERS August to September
SCENTED No
ASPECT Any, in a sheltered position; partial to full shade
SOIL Any fertile, moist, well-drained soil; prefers acid to neutral conditions
HARDINESS Fully hardy at temperatures down to -15°C/5°F; needs no winter protection
DROUGHT TOLERANCE Poor
PROBLEMS Slugs and snails; stem rot; resents disturbance
CARE Mulch annually with organic matter in spring
PROPAGATION Division in spring; sow ripe seed immediately in pots in a cold frame

Geranium phaeum
Mourning widow

⬆ 80cm/32in ↔ 45cm/18in   **EASY**

I have an incredible fondness for this geranium. It is a clump-forming hardy herbaceous perennial with deeply divided mid-green leaves, often with brown mottling, but it is the flowers that are so captivating. They are held above the leaves on slender branched stems and have reflexed petals of a deep purple-brown, with pale creamy centres, and curious curling, red stamens. It is not as showy as many of its counterparts, but it has muted, understated elegance. It happily self-seeds around the garden, but is never invasive.

BEST USES Ideal in a cottage garden and in both informal and formal beds and borders; does well in a lightly shaded woodland garden as ground cover

FLOWERS May to July
SCENTED No
ASPECT Any, in a sheltered or exposed position; full sun to partial shade
SOIL Any fertile, moist, well-drained soil
HARDINESS Fully hardy at temperatures down to -15°C/5°F; needs no winter protection
DROUGHT TOLERANCE Excellent, once established
PROBLEMS None
CARE Remove spent blooms after flowering; cut back leaves and stems to just above ground level in early spring
PROPAGATION Self-seeds easily; division in spring

Gillenia trifoliata ♀
Bowman's root/Indian physic

⬆ 90cm/3ft ↔ 60cm/24in   EASY

If you are looking for a tall, airy plant to fill a tricky gap in a shady border, look no further. This North American offering is a graceful, upright perennial with serrated bright green leaves, which have the good grace to flush claret in autumn. Willowy burgundy stems hold clusters of dainty, single, spidery star-shaped, white to pinkish flowers, with reddish calyces, high above the leaves. The skeletal seed heads in winter are a bonus. A much under-rated plant for all seasons. This seems to be the only garden variety on offer.

BEST USES A lovely plant for just about any border; good in a woodland garden or shady corner where the flowers will offer a ray of lightness to the shadows; ideal for naturalising in dappled shade with ornamental grasses; good as a cut flower

FLOWERS June

SCENTED No

ASPECT South, east or west facing, in a sheltered position; full sun (with shade protection at midday) to partial shade

SOIL Any fertile, well-drained soil; best with slight acidity

HARDINESS Fully hardy at temperatures down to -15°C/5°F; needs no winter protection

DROUGHT TOLERANCE Poor

PROBLEMS Slugs and snails

CARE Mulch the base of the plant with organic matter annually in early spring; stake in spring

PROPAGATION Division in autumn or spring; sow seed in pots in a cold frame in autumn or spring

Helenium 'Sahin's Early Flowerer' ♀

⬆ 90cm/3ft ↔ 60cm/24in   EASY

Originating in the Americas, this erect, clump-forming herbaceous perennial is ideal for bringing bold colour into the late-summer border. It has lance-shaped mid-green leaves, giving rise to sturdy branching stems that bear a plethora of rayed, daisy-like rich red flowers that develop orange streaking, with pronounced toast-brown centres. *H.* 'Butterpat' ♀ has gorgeous, dazzling golden yellow flowers; *H.* 'Moerheim Beauty' ♀ has coppery red flowers, fading to dusky orange with age; *H.* 'Bruno', with deep red flowers, and *H.* 'Waltraut' ♀, with vibrant rayed orange flowers with yellow edging, are both taller (1.2m/4ft).

BEST USES Perfect in the formal border or cottage garden; combines well with ornamental grasses in naturalistic planting schemes; hugely appealing to bees and butterflies; excellent as a cut flower

FLOWERS July to September

SCENTED No

ASPECT South, east or west facing, in a sheltered or exposed position; full sun

SOIL Any fertile, moist, well-drained soil

HARDINESS Fully hardy at temperatures down to -15°C/5°F; needs no winter protection

DROUGHT TOLERANCE Good, once established

PROBLEMS None

CARE May need staking; deadhead spent blooms to prolong the flowering

PROPAGATION Division every three to four years, in autumn or spring

Hemerocallis 'Whichford' ♀
Day lily

↑ 80cm/32in ↔ 50cm/20in   **EASY**

These evergreen or semi-evergreen clump-forming herbaceous perennials of Asian origin have a dazzling array of flower colours, ranging from white, orange, yellow and purple to red, and their strappy, vivid green foliage makes them a definite plus in the border nine months of the year. This cultivar bears elegant branched stems of large, fragrant, pale lemon yellow flared trumpets, flushed green at the throat, from mid-summer. Each bloom lasts only a day, but in the morning another lovely flower takes its place. Others include the rare H. 'Black Ice' (spidery burgundy flowers); H. 'Gentle Shepherd' (white); H. 'Saintly' (apricot); and H. 'Smoky Mountain Autumn' (rose).

BEST USES Wonderful with ornamental grasses, and in formal or informal borders; does fabulously well in containers; rabbit proof

FLOWERS June to July
SCENTED Yes
ASPECT South, east or west facing, in a sheltered or exposed position; full sun
SOIL Any fertile, well-drained, moist soil
HARDINESS Fully hardy at temperatures down to -15°C/5°F; needs no winter protection
DROUGHT TOLERANCE Good, once established
PROBLEMS None
CARE Deadhead daily; cut stems to the ground when flowering is over; mulch with organic matter in spring
PROPAGATION Division in autumn or spring

Hesperis matronalis
Sweet rocket

↑ 90cm/3ft ↔ 45cm/18in   **EASY**

This short-lived, clump-forming perennial, found from Asia and Russia to central Europe, has narrow, mid-green leaves on erect green stems topped with domed clusters of fragrant, simple, clove-like, four-petalled flowers, ranging in colour from purple to pale lilac-white in early summer. You will never see a plant without its full complement of pollen-collecting visitors. There is a fragrant white-flowered version, H.m. var. albiflora.

BEST USES Ideal in cottage gardens or wildflower gardens; also thrives in lightly shaded woodland gardens or in containers for city gardeners

FLOWERS May to July
SCENTED Yes
ASPECT South, east or west facing, in a sheltered or exposed position; full sun to partial shade
SOIL Any fertile, well-drained soil
HARDINESS Fully hardy/borderline at temperatures down to -15°C/5°F; may need winter protection in colder areas
DROUGHT TOLERANCE Good, once established
PROBLEMS Caterpillars, slugs and snails; powdery mildew
CARE Remove spent flowering stems; replace plants approximately every three years
PROPAGATION Self-seeds easily

Iris 'Sultan's Palace' (TB)

🡑 80cm/32in ⬌ 50cm/20in   **MEDIUM**

Irises are loved for their huge colour spectrum and the extravagance of their bearded flowers, which are often scented. There is a wide height range, from tiny alpine plants (10cm/4in) to the more statuesque water irises (up to 1.5m/5ft). However, for me it is the summer-flowering border irises with all the flamboyance of flamenco dancers that prove so captivating. This bulbous perennial is a Tall Bearded iris, and has sword-like green leaves and tall, smooth, sturdy stems, each bearing a sumptuous, fragrant, coppery velvet flower, with maroon falls, with flushed apricot throats. I. 'Mer du Sud' (TB) ♉ (90cm/3ft) has azure blue flowers.

> **BEST USES** This one's ideal for coastal gardeners; provides opulent colour in formal borders or gravel gardens; excellent as cut flowers

FLOWERS May to June
SCENTED Scented flowers
ASPECT South or west facing, in a sheltered position; full sun
SOIL Any fertile, moist, well-drained soil
HARDINESS Fully hardy at temperatures down to -15°C/5°F; needs no winter protection
DROUGHT TOLERANCE Poor
PROBLEMS Slugs and snails
CARE Remove a third of the top leaves when planting to help establish; mulch with organic matter in spring; cut back after flowering, every three years or so
PROPAGATION Division in autumn

Knautia macedonica

🡑 80cm/32in ⬌ 45cm/18in   **EASY**

This unassuming, clump-forming herbaceous perennial from the Balkans is a simple plant, but no less lovely for its uncontrived charm. It has serrated mid-green leaves and slender, wiry, branching green stems producing small, very free-flowering, button-like bristly flowers, the colour of mulled wine, that colour up best in full sun. K. arvensis (field scabious) is much taller at 1.5m/5ft, with similar pincushion, pale lilac-blue flowers.

> **BEST USES** Marvellous in the wildflower or cottage garden, and bees and insects love it; associates well amongst grasses, where its pretty flower heads can be best appreciated

FLOWERS July to September
SCENTED No
ASPECT South, east or west facing, in a sheltered or exposed position; full sun to partial shade (flowering is reduced in shade)
SOIL Any fertile, well-drained soil
HARDINESS Fully hardy at temperatures down to -15°C/5°F; needs no winter protection
DROUGHT TOLERANCE Excellent, once established
PROBLEMS Aphids; powdery mildew
CARE Mulch with organic matter annually in spring; may need staking; cut down to ground level in autumn
PROPAGATION Division in autumn or spring; sow seed in pots in a cold frame in spring

Leucanthemum vulgare
Ox-eye daisy

↑ 90cm/3ft ↔ 50cm/20in   **EASY**

This European rhizomatous clump-forming herbaceous perennial is commonly sighted in meadows and roadsides in the UK. It has dark green, spoon-shaped leaves and bears single, daisy-like flowers (2.5–5cm/1–2in across) with white rayed petals radiating from cheerful yellow centres. It may never win an award, but it is a prolific flowerer over a long period, does well in almost any soil and needs very little attention.

> **BEST USES** Invaluable in the wildflower garden or meadow as it is loved by pollinating insects; does well in flower borders; deserves a whirl in containers as it flowers for a long period

FLOWERS May to September

SCENTED No

ASPECT Any, in a sheltered or exposed position; full sun to partial shade

SOIL Any fertile, well-drained soil

HARDINESS Fully hardy at temperatures down to -15°C/5°F; needs no winter protection

DROUGHT TOLERANCE Good, once established

PROBLEMS Aphids

CARE May need staking; remove spent flower stems to prevent self-seeding; cut back to just above ground level in winter; mulch with organic matter annually in spring

PROPAGATION Division in spring

• •

GREENFINGER TIP *To avoid the need for staking, grow them with other sturdier, supportive perennials*

Lunaria rediviva
Perennial honesty

↑ 90cm/3ft ↔ 60cm/24in   **EASY**

Honesty can be found in neglected meadows of Europe and may be a biennial (often grown as an annual) or, like this one, a short-lived clump-forming herbaceous perennial. It is best known for its tall stems, with branching heart-shaped leaves and distinctive flat, disc-like ghostly silver seed pods. This variety has typical rounded, serrated, tapering mid-green leaves, and bears tall, slender, smooth, green branching stems with masses of lightly fragrant tiny pale purple flowers, held in lacy panicles, from late spring to summer.

> **BEST USES** Ideal in a woodland or cottage garden, where it will make a thriving colony in no time; the pearly seed cases make excellent dried flowers

FLOWERS May to August

SCENTED Yes

ASPECT Any, in a sheltered position; full sun to partial shade

SOIL Any fertile, moist, well-drained soil

HARDINESS Fully hardy at temperatures down to -15°C/5°F; needs no winter protection

DROUGHT TOLERANCE Good, once established

PROBLEMS Clubroot

CARE Remove spent flowers before seed heads are formed if you don't want them to self-seed

PROPAGATION Self-seeds easily; sow seed in situ in late spring

Lupinus 'The Governor' (Band of Nobles Series)

⬆ 90cm/3ft ⬌ 50cm/20in   **MEDIUM**

Lupins are members of the pea family from the Mediterranean and Africa. These clump-forming perennials have elegant, tapering spires (up to 60cm/24in long) of pea-like single or bi-coloured flowers, opening from the bottom up, densely clustered up straight stems. This bushy variety, with palmate leaves of fresh green, produces tall, pepper-scented flower spikes of purple-blue and white. Choice bi-coloured varieties include *L.* 'Manhattan Lights' (blackcurrant and banana) and *L.* 'Tequila Flame' (raspberry red and custard). Single colours include *L.* 'Morello Cherry' (cherry red) and *L.* 'Desert Sun' (clear yellow).

> **BEST USES** Ideal for formal or cottage gardens; attractive to pollinating insects; does well in pots

FLOWERS June

SCENTED Yes

ASPECT South, east or west facing, in a sheltered position; full sun to partial shade

SOIL Any fertile, well-drained, slightly acid soil

HARDINESS Fully hardy at temperatures down to -15°C/5°F

DROUGHT TOLERANCE Poor

PROBLEMS Aphids, slugs and snails; fungal diseases

CARE Mulch with organic matter annually in spring; may need staking; deadhead to encourage a second flowering

PROPAGATION Sow pre-soaked seed at 15°C/59°F in spring; basal stem cuttings in spring

Monarda 'Cambridge Scarlet' 🎖

Bergamot

⬆ 90cm/3ft ⬌ 50cm/20in   **EASY**

This upright, clump-forming, rhizomatous perennial from North America makes a tall plant. Straight stems of large, exuberant, explosive, spidery, tufted scarlet red flowers rise above the oval, pointed dark green leaves, which are lemon-scented. *M.* 'Beauty of Cobham' 🎖 has pale pink flowers with red stems; *M.* 'Mahogany' has deep claret flowers, and *M.* 'Mohawk', with good mildew resistance, has pale lilac-purple flowers; all are 90cm/3ft tall.

> **BEST USES** A vivid addition to any border; wonderful with the shorter ornamental grasses, so will suit a prairie planting scheme; ideal for the wildlife garden because pollinating insects love it

FLOWERS July to September

SCENTED Aromatic leaves

ASPECT South, east or west facing, in a sheltered position; full sun to partial shade

SOIL Any fertile, moist, humus-rich, well-drained soil

HARDINESS Fully hardy at temperatures down to -15°C/5°F; needs no winter protection

DROUGHT TOLERANCE Poor

PROBLEMS Slugs and snails; powdery mildew

CARE Mulch with organic matter annually in spring; cut back spent flower spikes

PROPAGATION Division in spring before new growth starts

PEONIES

They say if you grow a peony, you have it for life.

Herbaceous peonies (not to be confused with the shrubby tree peonies from the same family) are tuberous, clump-forming perennials from Europe and Asia, with fine foliage and sumptuous blooms.

They have large, showy, saucer-shaped to deeply cupped single, double or anemone-like flowers, usually borne on single stems, though some varieties can bear numerous flower buds per stem. Many cultivars are fragrant and the lobed leaves are an attractive feature, making appealing clumps even when not in flower, and often flushed red in autumn.

Herbaceous peonies have a short flowering season, in early to mid-summer, and range in height from 50cm/20in to more than 90cm/3ft, with flower colour varying from white, pink, red, yellow and numerous pastel shades in between.

Peonies dislike disturbance and often fail to flower the season after they have been divided. Mulch them well after division. That said, my *P.l.* 'Sarah Bernhardt' – *see above* – flowered again immediately, but others I have moved sulked and made me wait a year.

Among the many varieties, *P. tennifolia* (70cm/28in) has deep red flowers from late spring; *P. wittmanniana* (90cm/3ft) has gorgeous pale lemon single flowers in early summer; *P.* 'Red Charm' (up to 90cm/3ft) has fragrant, deep velvet-red flowers from early to mid-summer; *P.* 'Eden's Perfume' (75cm/30in) has frothy pink flowers in early summer.

Paeonia lactiflora 'Duchesse de Nemours' ♥

⬆ 90cm/3ft ⬌ 90cm/3ft   **EASY**

Peonies are large, clump-forming perennials that grow as tall as they do wide, and are famed for their fleeting, but glorious, glamorous summer flowers. Supporting the heavy flowers without shirking, this variety makes a large glossy mound of pointed, polished, deep green leaves in smart, appealing clumps. But it is the sweetly fragrant, deeply cupped double flowers of purest unblemished ivory, with tightly crinkled petals, that make it the pick of the peony bunch. *P.l* 'Sarah Bernhardt' ♥ has fragrant, double, soft pink flowers but is not as self-supporting; *P.l.* 'Adolphe Rousseau' has scented, double, deep red flowers; *P.l.* 'Kelway's Glorious' has deeply fragrant, double flowers that are white, tinted crimson.

BEST USES Excellent in a large, formal border; a mainstay in a cottage garden; great as cut flowers

FLOWERS June to July

SCENTED Scented flowers

ASPECT South or west facing, in a sheltered position; full sun

SOIL Any fertile, moist, well-drained soil

HARDINESS Fully hardy at temperatures down to -15°C/5°F; needs no winter protection

DROUGHT TOLERANCE Poor

PROBLEMS Peony wilt

CARE Most peonies need staking, but not this one; deadhead spent blooms; mulch with organic matter annually in spring

PROPAGATION Division in autumn or early spring

Papaver orientale 'Patty's Plum'
Oriental poppy

⬆ 70cm/28in ⬌ 90cm/3ft   **EASY**

Originally from Turkey and northern Iran, Oriental poppies are clump-forming herbaceous perennials. This variety is clothed with deeply lobed silvery green leaves (up to 30cm/12in long) and strong, bristly stems. From early to mid-summer, fat, round, apple-tinted flower buds burst to reveal extravagant, tissue-papered, faded, silky blackcurrant-coloured flowers, the size of saucers; inside you will see four black smudges and heavily mascaraed stamens. Each bloom lasts only three or four days, but they are a joy to behold. *P.o.* 'Leuchtfeuer' ♥ has shaggy-edged blooms of vivid orange; *P.o.* 'Perry's White' has white petals with black centres.

> **BEST USES** Lovely as a splash of colour for the cottage or formal border; naturalises well with grasses or airy plants in the middle of the flower bed

FLOWERS May to July

SCENTED No

ASPECT South or west facing, in a sheltered position; full sun

SOIL Any fertile, moist, well-drained soil

HARDINESS Fully hardy at temperatures down to -15°C/5°F; needs no winter protection

DROUGHT TOLERANCE Good, once established

PROBLEMS Aphids; downy mildew

CARE Stake when planting to support flowers; mulch with organic matter annually in spring

PROPAGATION Division in spring; sow seed in spring; root cuttings in winter

Phlomis russeliana ♥
Jerusalem sage

⬆ 90cm/3ft ⬌ 1.5m/5ft   **EASY**

Phlomis are a family of sage-like shrubs and perennials thriving in rocky areas in Europe to Africa and Asia, so are good for hot, dry, sunny spots. This vigorous, upright, clump-forming, semi-evergreen perennial from southern Europe has large, hairy, pointed oval, olive green aromatic leaves making large mounds and sends up tall, stiff stems that have whorled clusters of hooded, pale yellow flowers sparsely studding their length. It is a plant of parched pale yellow perfection. The brown seed heads cling to the stems in crusty balls, making them an interesting autumn feature.

> **BEST USES** A good focal point in the summer border; blends well in Mediterranean, gravel or prairie borders; bees love it, so good for wildflower gardens

FLOWERS July to August

SCENTED Aromatic leaves

ASPECT South, east or west facing, in a sheltered or exposed position; full sun

SOIL Any fertile, moist, well-drained soil

HARDINESS Fully hardy at temperatures down to -15°C/5°F; needs no winter protection

DROUGHT TOLERANCE Good, once established

PROBLEMS Leafhoppers

CARE Cut back dead or damaged growth in spring

PROPAGATION Division in spring

Potentilla atrosanguinea
Cinquefoil

⬆ 80cm/32in ⬌ 60cm/24in   **EASY**

This Himalayan clump-forming perennial adds a dash of vibrant colour to the border. It has dark green-grey, hairy leaves with serrated edges, similar to strawberry foliage (they are related). In summer to autumn it sends up wiry, sage-coloured, branching stems bearing clusters of bright red to orange flowers, all with bright yellow eyes and lash-like yellow stamens. *P.a.* var. *argyrophylla* (45cm/18in) has deep green leaves and vivid saffron blooms with flushed orange centres.

BEST USES An ideal border plant that is easy to grow, low maintenance and perfect for lively colour and appealing foliage; grow in containers to add exotic colour to a sunny courtyard or city patio

FLOWERS July to September
SCENTED No
ASPECT South, east or west facing, in a sheltered position; full sun
SOIL Any fertile, well-drained soil
HARDINESS Fully hardy at temperatures down to -15°C/5°F; needs no winter protection
DROUGHT TOLERANCE Poor
PROBLEMS None
CARE Mulch with organic matter annually in spring; trim after flowering
PROPAGATION Division in autumn or spring; sow seed in pots in a cold frame in autumn or spring

Salvia × sylvestris 'Mainacht' ⚇
Wood sage

⬆ 80cm/32in ⬌ 30cm/12in   **EASY**

Salvias can be annuals, perennials or shrubs and are originally from both temperate and tropical regions worldwide. This upright, clump-forming hybrid is one of the best perennial salvias, with dark green, bristly, aromatic leaves that make pleasing clumps and erect, elegant, vibrantly coloured spires of the most glorious lipped, hooded, small, deep rich indigo blue flowers (up to 8cm/3in long), arranged in circular whorls around each stem. Other notable varieties include *S. × s.* 'Rose Queen' (75cm/30in), with rose pink flowers, and *S. × s.* 'Blauhügel' ⚇ (50cm/20in) with violet-blue flowers.

BEST USES A lovely addition to the Mediterranean or gravel garden and the traditional border; does well in coastal gardens; bees and butterflies love it

FLOWERS June to July
SCENTED Aromatic leaves
ASPECT South or west facing, in a sheltered position; full sun
SOIL Any fertile, moist, well-drained soil
HARDINESS Fully hardy/borderline at temperatures down to -15°C/5°F; may need winter protection in colder areas
DROUGHT TOLERANCE Poor
PROBLEMS Slugs and snails
CARE Remove spent flower spikes to prolong flowering
PROPAGATION Division in spring; basal stem or stem-tip cuttings in spring to early summer

Solidago × *luteus* 'Lemore' ♀

⬆ 90cm/3ft ⬌ 30cm/12in　　　　EASY

A neat, low-growing, slightly arching, clump-forming perennial, this is a cross (hybrid) between *Solidago* (Golden rod) and an aster. It produces an abundance of loose-branched sprays of daisy-like pale creamy lemon flowers, in late summer to early autumn. To my mind, the flower colour is far superior to the usual yellow offering of Golden rod and it is more restrained in habit, so ideal for smaller spaces.

BEST USES Ideal for the Mediterranean garden or cottage garden border; good for wildflower gardens, as it is attractive to pollinating insects

FLOWERS July to September

SCENTED No

ASPECT South, east or west facing, in a sheltered position; full sun to partial shade

SOIL Any fertile, well-drained soil

HARDINESS Fully hardy at temperatures down to -15°C/5°F; needs no winter protection

DROUGHT TOLERANCE Poor

PROBLEMS Powdery mildew

CARE Mulch with organic matter annually in spring; cutting the flowers prolongs the flowering period

PROPAGATION Division in spring; sow seed at 15°C/59°F in a greenhouse in spring

Tanacetum coccineum 'Brenda'
Tansy

⬆ 80cm/32in ⬌ 45cm/18in　　　　EASY

Just one look at the vibrant colour of this bushy, herbaceous perennial suggests it is of Mediterranean origin. It's related to the aster family and has finely dissected, ferny basal leaves of bright green, from which emerge tall, thin, bare stems, topped with single daisy-like flowers (up to 8cm/3in across) of the most flamboyant magenta, with dark yellow centres. It looks dainty but is as tough as they come: unfussy about soil, the only thing that seems to kill it is waterlogging. *T.c.* 'Eileen May Robinson' ♀ (90cm/3ft) has pale, soft pink flowers; *T.c.* 'James Kelway' ♀ (60cm/24in) has bright red flowers; *T.c.* 'Snow Cloud' (60cm/24in) has white flowers.

BEST USES A lovely addition to the Mediterranean or gravel garden as well as the more traditional border; good for coastal gardens

FLOWERS June to July

SCENTED No

ASPECT South or west facing, in a sheltered position; full sun

SOIL Any fertile, well-drained soil

HARDINESS Fully hardy at temperatures down to -15°C/5°F; needs no winter protection

DROUGHT TOLERANCE Poor

PROBLEMS Aphids

CARE Cut back hard after the flowers fade to encourage a second flush of flowering

PROPAGATION Division in spring; basal stem cuttings in spring

Thalictrum aquilegiifolium 'Thundercloud'

⬆ 90cm/3ft ◀▶ 45cm/18in   **EASY**

A clump-forming rhizomatous perennial, found from Asia to Europe, with a graceful, upright, branching, airy habit, this is a lovely plant for shady places. It has scalloped mid-green leaves and sends up tall, slender purple stems, bearing branching sprays of masses of tiny, delicate, fluffy, rayed, faded purple flowers with dark purple stamens (but doesn't actually have petals to speak of). *T. aquilegiifolium* (90cm/3ft) has pale mauve flowers.

BEST USES A gauzy plant that is uplifting in a woodland garden or adding airy grace to a slightly gloomy border; excellent for wildlife gardens as bees and butterflies love it

FLOWERS June to August
SCENTED No
ASPECT East or west facing, in a sheltered position; partial shade
SOIL Any fertile, moist, humus-rich, well-drained soil
HARDINESS Fully hardy at temperatures down to -15°C/5°F; needs no winter protection
DROUGHT TOLERANCE Poor
PROBLEMS Slugs and snails; powdery mildew
CARE Mulch with organic matter annually in spring; may need staking, as is liable to keel over; cut back faded flower stems
PROPAGATION Division in spring, as new growth starts (mulch after division); sow ripe seed immediately in pots in a cold frame

Thermopsis rhombifolia var. montana
False lupin

⬆ 90cm/3ft ◀▶ 60cm/24in   **EASY**

A spreading, rhizomatous perennial that originates in mountain areas and grassy woodlands in the USA and Mexico, which gives some indication of the growing conditions it enjoys, this has fresh green, tri-palmate leaves with undersides covered in fine silken hairs. It sends up tall, upright, dark greeny charcoal stems that produce spires of pea-like, zingy sulphur yellow flowers. It is unfussy about soil type but has a tendency to invasiveness.

BEST USES Excellent for coastal gardens; ideal for the wildlife garden as it is an effective butterfly lure

FLOWERS May to July
SCENTED No
ASPECT South, east or west facing, in a sheltered or exposed position; full sun to partial shade
SOIL Any fertile, well-drained soil
HARDINESS Fully hardy at temperatures down to -15°C/5°F; needs no winter protection
DROUGHT TOLERANCE Good, once established
PROBLEMS Slugs and snails nibble young foliage
CARE Cut back flower stems after flowering
PROPAGATION Division in spring or summer (but plants resent disturbance and can take time to recover); better to sow seed at a minimum temperature of 10°C/50°F in spring

GREENFINGER TIP *This is a viable alternative to border lupins, being less prone to aphid attack, but it lacks the colour spectrum of traditional lupins*

Aconitum 'Spark's Variety' ♎
Monkshood

⬆ 1.2–1.5m/4–5ft ⬌ 45cm/18in   **EASY**

Aconitums are (usually) tuberous perennials found in alpine meadows and mountainous scrub across the northern hemisphere and the flowers are generally blue or purple. This upright, clump-forming perennial has large, deeply lobed, ornamental dark green leaves and strong, self-supporting, stiff, tall stems carrying panicles of hooded, deep violet flowers (each up to 5cm/2in across) on slim, branching stems. Monkshood comes into its own in late summer, offering height, strong foliage shape and colour to the late-summer border. *A.* 'Stainless Steel' has metallic, ice blue flowers; *A.* 'Ivorine' is more compact (90cm/3ft), with creamy white flowers. (All parts are poisonous; leaves can irritate skin.)

BEST USES Indispensable for the woodland garden or shady formal border; repeat at intervals to knit together a planting composition harmoniously

FLOWERS July to August
SCENTED No
ASPECT Any; partial shade
SOIL Any fertile, humus-rich, well-drained soil
HARDINESS Fully hardy at temperatures down to -15°C/5°F; needs no winter protection
DROUGHT TOLERANCE Poor
PROBLEMS Aphids; stem rot and *Verticillium* wilt
CARE Mulch with organic matter annually in spring to conserve moisture, especially on a sunny site
PROPAGATION Division every three years in autumn to late winter (can be slow to re-establish)

Agapanthus 'Blue Giant'
African blue lily

⬆ 1.2m/4ft ⬌ 60cm/24in   **EASY**

Agapanthus originate in South Africa and are showy, clump-forming, rhizomatous herbaceous perennials with fresh strap-like leaves. This deciduous to semi-evergreen variety has tall, smooth, sturdy stems bearing large, clear azure blue globes, made up of myriad smaller star-shaped flowers. *A.* 'Midnight Star' (60cm/24in) is shorter and well worth growing for its rich dark blue flowers; *A.* 'Blue Heaven' (75cm/30in) is paler blue, flowering from June to September; *A.* 'Bressingham White' (90cm/3ft) has white flowers, tipped pale pink.

BEST USES Ideal as vertical accents in the summer border or gravel garden; grows very well in containers and coastal gardens; irresistible to pollinating insects

FLOWERS July to August
SCENTED No
ASPECT South, east or west facing, in a sheltered position; full sun
SOIL Any fertile, moist, well-drained soil
HARDINESS Fully hardy/borderline at temperatures down to -15°C/5°F; may need winter protection in colder areas
DROUGHT TOLERANCE Good, once established
PROBLEMS Slugs and snails
CARE Mulch with organic matter in spring; protect crowns with a dry mulch in colder regions in winter
PROPAGATION Division in spring (ensure roots don't dry out when transplanting)

Ageratina altissima 'Chocolate' ♈

(formerly *Eupatorium rugosum* 'Chocolate')

⬆ 1.5m/5ft ⬌ 60cm/24in   **EASY**

Only consider these tall, erect, bushy, clump-forming North American perennials (commonly known as White snakeroot) if you have a large garden. This showy variety has nettle-like lance-shaped leaves that are green, flushed chocolate, on sturdy purple stems, with profuse clusters of foamy, fluffy white flowers from summer to early autumn.

> **BEST USES** A statuesque plant for larger spaces; happy in a large mixed border in a formal or cottage garden; thrives in a damp wild garden or by the water's edge; attractive to bees and butterflies

FLOWERS July to September

SCENTED No

ASPECT North, east or west facing, in a sheltered or exposed position; partial shade

SOIL Any fertile, moist soil

HARDINESS Fully hardy at temperatures down to -15°C/5°F; needs no winter protection

DROUGHT TOLERANCE Poor

PROBLEMS Aphids, slugs and snails

CARE May need staking; cut spent flower stems down to ground level; dry mulch crowns to prevent frost damage to new shoots

PROPAGATION Division in spring

Angelica sylvestris 'Purpurea'

Purple angelica

⬆ 1.7m/5½ft ⬌ 90cm/3ft   **EASY**

I am particularly fond of this statuesque, short-lived herbaceous perennial (or biennial), which is the purple version of our native wild angelica. It has very attractive, deeply divided purple leaves and sends up tall, upright, smooth damson-coloured stems. These are topped with tightly branched domes of deep pink flower buds that open to creamy pink flowers, 20cm/8in across, but it is worth growing for the foliage alone. *A. archangelica* (2m/6ft) has green leaves and stems and acid yellow flower heads in early summer, and is better for north-facing borders.

> **BEST USES** Excellent as a late focal point in the formal flower border; adored by bees, butterflies and hoverflies, so ideal for the wildflower garden

FLOWERS August to September

SCENTED No

ASPECT South, east or west facing, in a sheltered or exposed position; full sun

SOIL Any fertile, moist, well-drained soil

HARDINESS Fully hardy at temperatures down to -15°C/5°F; needs no winter protection

DROUGHT TOLERANCE Poor

PROBLEMS Aphids, leaf miners, slugs and snails; powdery mildew

CARE Mulch with organic matter annually in spring; remove faded flower heads, unless you are collecting seed

PROPAGATION Sow ripe seed immediately (using rootrainers as they don't transplant well)

Campanula lactiflora 'Loddon Anna' ♍
Milky bellflower

⬆ 1.5m/5ft ↔ 60cm/24in   **EASY**

This hardy herbaceous perennial, found across the northern hemisphere, has an upright, clump-forming habit. Fairly sturdy, sparsely clothed, branching stems emerge from the leaf base of coarse, toothed, pointed mid-green leaves, and hold clusters of pale, soft pink-lilac, star-shaped, single, five-petalled flowers. Campanulas are sometimes known as the poor man's delphinium because they have a similar habit but are happy in shade. *C.l.* 'Avalanche' (1.2m/4ft), with white flowers, flowers very freely in summer; *C.l.* 'Prichard's Variety' ♍ (90cm/3ft) is slightly more compact, with elegant violet-blue flowers.

> **BEST USES** Ideal at the back of a formal or cottage garden; the flower colour is more intense in light shade, so it is perfect for a dappled spot

FLOWERS July to September
SCENTED No
ASPECT Any, in a sheltered position; full sun to partial shade
SOIL Any fertile, moist, well-drained soil
HARDINESS Fully hardy at temperatures down to -15°C/5°F; needs no winter protection
DROUGHT TOLERANCE Poor
PROBLEMS Aphids; powdery mildew and rust
CARE Cut back spent flower stems to limit self-seeding
PROPAGATION Self-seeds easily; division in autumn or spring; sow seed in pots in a cold frame in spring

Canna 'Wyoming' ♍
Indian shot plant

⬆ 2m/6ft ↔ 50cm/20in   **MEDIUM**

Cannas are tall, rhizomatous herbaceous perennials, from the tropics to Asia, grown for their very large, highly ornamental leathery leaves, that vary from green to purples, often with appealing pronounced veining, and gladioli-like flowers in reds, oranges and yellows. They are showy plants and not for the faint-hearted. C. 'Wyoming' is a tall, upright plant that has dark purple leaves, etched with even deeper purple veins, and warm, orange flowers. C. 'Lucifer' (60cm/24in) has green leaves and red flowers, with yellow edging; C. 'Richard Wallace' (1.5m/5ft) has yellow flowers.

> **BEST USES** Excellent for colour impact in a hot coloured or exotic border; ideal for large containers in a contemporary city garden

FLOWERS June to September
SCENTED No
ASPECT South or west facing, in a sheltered position; full sun
SOIL Any fertile, well-drained soil
HARDINESS Half hardy at temperatures down to 0°C/32°F; needs winter protection
DROUGHT TOLERANCE Excellent, once established
PROBLEMS Caterpillars, slugs and snails
CARE In warm areas, cover with a dry mulch of leaves; in colder areas, lift, store and replant the following year after all risk of frost has passed
PROPAGATION Division of rhizomes in early spring

Cephalaria gigantea
Yellow scabious

⬆ 2.5m/8ft ⬄ 60cm/24in   **EASY**

This clump-forming perennial of Turkish origin looks like a large scabious (not surprisingly, as it's a relative). It has rough, narrow, lanced green leaves, arranged fairly sparsely on very tall, wiry stems that are topped with plenty of delightful lemon yellow pincushion flowers (about 6cm/2½in across). There are few other varieties worth mentioning.

> **BEST USES** Excellent on heavy, poor-draining clay but won't tolerate dry soil; good for the wildflower garden as it is loved by bees and butterflies

FLOWERS June to August
SCENTED No
ASPECT Any, in a sheltered or exposed position; full sun
SOIL Fertile, moist, well-drained soil
HARDINESS Fully hardy at temperatures down to -15°C/5°F; needs no winter protection
DROUGHT TOLERANCE Poor
PROBLEMS None
CARE Mulch with organic matter annually in spring; may need staking; cut back after flowering (and cut back to the base in spring)
PROPAGATION Division in early to mid-spring; sow seed in pots in a cold frame in spring

•••
GREENFINGER TIP *Scabious can get a bit sprawly, so grow this next to sturdier perennials that will offer support*

Crambe cordifolia ♗
Great sea kale

⬆ 2.5m/8ft ⬄ 1.5m/5ft   **EASY**

Originally from Europe, this stunning, architectural clump-forming perennial has large, rounded to oval, heavily veined, bristly green leaves, but it's the frothy mass of tiny, scented, foamy white flowers, on slender, very widely branching stems, that really catches your eye: once in full flower, the large billowing cloud of fragrant white flowers almost eclipses the leaves. It takes up a lot of space for such a fleeting confection, but if you have the room, the sheer joyful abundance is worth it.

> **BEST USES** Ideal at the back of a wide, sunny border with dark purples or hot colours planted alongside; at home in the cottage garden and informal wildflower garden; bees and insects love it

FLOWERS June to July
SCENTED Lightly scented flowers
ASPECT South, east or west facing, in a sheltered position, protected from cold winds; full sun to partial shade
SOIL Any fertile, well-drained soil; short-lived on heavy soil
HARDINESS Fully hardy at temperatures down to -15°C/5°F; needs no winter protection
DROUGHT TOLERANCE Excellent, once established
PROBLEMS Slugs and snails may be a nuisance in spring; the leaves grow tatty with age
CARE Cut back to ground level in autumn
PROPAGATION Sow seed at 10°C/50°F in pots in a cold frame in spring; root cuttings in late autumn

Crinum × powellii ♉

⬆ 1.5m/5ft ⬌ 30cm/12in   **EASY**

This heavenly bulbous South African perennial has light green, arching strap-like leaves and produces spectacular large trumpets of fragrant pale pink flowers on tall, smooth, straight, stiff stems from late summer into early autumn. It is not generally regarded as drought tolerant but, given a humus-rich soil from the outset, it will do pretty well. *C. × p.* 'Album' ♉ has white flowers.

BEST USES Ideal for bringing vertical shapes and colour into the late-summer and autumn border; excellent in large containers (it likes a restricted root run) on a sunny patio

FLOWERS August to September

SCENTED Scented flowers

ASPECT South, east or west facing, in a sheltered position; full sun

SOIL Any fertile, moist, humus-rich, well-drained soil

HARDINESS Fully hardy/borderline at temperatures down to -15°C/5°F; may need winter protection in colder areas

DROUGHT TOLERANCE Good, once established

PROBLEMS None

CARE Plant new bulbs with the tips just showing above the soil; mulch with organic matter annually in spring

PROPAGATION Pot up rooted offsets in spring

. . . .

GREENFINGER TIP *Keep the roots congested and don't divide them too early in their career: they will flower more profusely if left undisturbed*

Cynara cardunculus ♉
Cardoon

⬆ 1.5m/5ft ⬌ 1.2m/4ft   **EASY**

This very tall, erect Mediterranean perennial is a large, architectural plant that is not for the faint-hearted. It has strong, thick, woolly stems with large, deeply divided, prickly, grey-silver leaves (up to 50cm/20in long). Large thistle-like, honey-scented purple flowers are produced in late summer (and look lovely touched with winter frost). *C.c.* Scolymus Group also has large silver leaves, but is usually grown for its edible flower buds.

BEST USES Makes a striking focal point in a gravel garden, in a wide sunny border or coastal garden; bees and butterflies love it

FLOWERS June to September

SCENTED Scented flowers

ASPECT South, east or west facing, in a sheltered position; full sun

SOIL Any fertile, well-drained soil

HARDINESS Fully hardy/borderline at temperatures down to -15°C/5°F; may need winter protection in colder areas

DROUGHT TOLERANCE Excellent, once established

PROBLEMS Aphids, slugs and snails; *Botrytis* (grey mould)

CARE Stake plants exposed to winds, using cable or rubber tree ties; cut back to ground level in winter and dry mulch the crown

PROPAGATION Division in spring; sow seed in pots in a cold frame in spring; root cuttings in winter

Delphinium 'Blue Nile' ♚

↑ 1.7m/5½ft ↔ 60–90cm/2–3ft   **MEDIUM**

Delphiniums are upright, clump-forming herbaceous perennials from mountainous regions worldwide that have become traditional cottage garden favourites. This typical example has attractively toothed dark green leaves (some 20cm/ 8in across) and tall, stately, steepled flower spikes studded with semi-double, bright to mid-blue flowers with white centres, from early to mid-summer. Other notable varieties are *D*. Black Knight Group (1.7m/5½ft), with elegant blue-black spires, and *D*. 'Sungleam' ♚ (2m/6ft), with buttery cream flowers. (Plants are toxic.)

BEST USES Essential in any self-respecting cottage garden and for elegant vertical accents in a formal summer border; excellent as cut flowers

FLOWERS June to July
SCENTED No
ASPECT South, east or west facing, in a sheltered position, with protection from cold winds; full sun
SOIL Any fertile, well-drained soil
HARDINESS Fully hardy at temperatures down to -15°C/5°F; needs no winter protection
DROUGHT TOLERANCE Poor
PROBLEMS Caterpillars, slugs and snails; crown rot, leaf spot and powdery mildew
CARE Mulch with organic matter in early spring; may need staking; remove spent flower spikes for a modest second flowering; cut back to ground level in autumn
PROPAGATION Sow seed in spring; basal stem cuttings in early spring

Dracunculus vulgaris
Stink lily/Voodoo lily

↑ 1.5m/5ft ↔ 60cm/24in   **EASY**

The name is certainly no enticement to grow this slightly tender tuberous perennial from the Mediterranean, but the flowers and foliage are spectacularly exotic. In spring a smooth, brown, mottled spike emerges from the ground and unfurls deeply jagged dark green leaves, often with white marbling. In summer, dramatic deep brown-maroon spathes, with loosely frilled edges, are displayed on stout stems, with a highly polished purple-black spadix arising from the centre. It has a strong odour, like the smell of rotting meat (and is pollinated by flies), but this only lasts a day or so and I have never found it overpowering enough to put me off.

BEST USES Adds spring and summer interest to the cottage garden or formal border; provides temporary ground cover in the shrub border; foliage provides visual impact in an exotic garden

FLOWERS June to July
SCENTED Unpleasant scent from spadix
ASPECT Any, in a sheltered position; full sun to full shade
SOIL Any fertile, well-drained soil
HARDINESS Frost hardy at temperatures down to -5°C/23°F; needs winter protection in colder areas
DROUGHT TOLERANCE Excellent, once established
PROBLEMS None
CARE Dry mulch the crown in winter
PROPAGATION Plant offsets in spring or autumn

Filipendula purpurea 🏅
Meadowsweet

⬆ 1.2m/4ft ⬌ 60cm/24in   **EASY**

Meadowsweet is an upright, clump-forming, spreading perennial from Japan with palm-like mid-green leaves, up to 25cm/10in across. Sweetly scented, plumed, fluffy, pinky red flowers, fading to pale pink, are carried high above the aromatic leaves on tall red-purple stems. It positively embraces poorly drained soil and the foliage makes such pleasing mounds that this is an infinitely useful plant. *F. purpurea* f. *albiflora* (40cm/16in) has white flowers; *F.p.* 'Elegans' (90cm/3ft) has rose pink flowers followed by attractive red-bronze seed heads.

BEST USES Ideal for planting in damp, poorly drained beds and borders, at the water's edge or in damp, boggy ground; suits cottage gardens; good deciduous ground cover in a woodland garden

FLOWERS July to August

SCENTED Scented flowers and leaves

ASPECT Any, in a sheltered or exposed position; full sun to partial shade

SOIL Any fertile, moist, humus-rich soil

HARDINESS Fully hardy at temperatures down to -15°C/5°F; needs no winter protection

DROUGHT TOLERANCE Poor

PROBLEMS Leaf spot and downy mildew in dry conditions

CARE Mulch with organic matter annually in spring to help conserve moisture in the soil

PROPAGATION Division in autumn or spring

Geranium psilostemon 🏅
Armenian cranesbill

⬆ 1.2m/4ft ⬌ 1.2m/4ft   **EASY**

I defy anyone not to love this plant. One of the mightier hardy geraniums, it is an energetic, clump-forming, herbaceous perennial, with appealing, larger than average, deeply lobed, dissected green-gold leaves that are red-tinted in autumn. It makes a large, loose, leafy mound, with slender, wiry branching flower stems of simple, five-petalled, vivid magenta flowers, with deep black eyes and damson veining on the petals. *G.* 'Ann Folkard' 🏅 (60cm/24in) has similar magenta flowers with dark centres, and yellow-green foliage, but is more restrained.

BEST USES Perfect for so many locations, from cottage gardens to long, wide borders; makes handsome ground cover underplanting a mixed shrub border or in a north-facing border (though flowering will be reduced)

FLOWERS June to August

SCENTED No

ASPECT Any, in a sheltered or exposed position; full sun to partial shade

SOIL Any fertile, well-drained soil

HARDINESS Fully hardy at temperatures down to -15°C/5°F; needs no winter protection

DROUGHT TOLERANCE Poor

PROBLEMS Powdery and downy mildew

CARE Needs staking; remove faded flower stems and any tatty leaves to encourage a second flush of flowers and new leafy growth

PROPAGATION Division in early spring

Gunnera manicata ♛
Chile rhubarb

⬆ 2.5m/8ft ⬌ 3–4m/10–13ft **MEDIUM**

Coming across this clump-forming South American rhizomatous perennial is a bit like wandering into *Jurassic Park*. The enormous, palmate, deeply veined, deeply jagged leaves (2m/6ft long) tower over your head, held aloft by thick, brawny, prickled stems, up to 2.5m/8ft tall. Branching cones of greenish, flushed red, flower heads (about 90cm/3ft long) are produced in early summer, giving way to curious round, green fruits. It needs space and gallons of water. *G. tinctoria* ♛ (1.5m/5ft) looks similar but is more manageable.

BEST USES Give it pride of place in a large border or damp woodland, with lots of humus (and a hose pipe near by); ideal by a pond, stream or ditch

FLOWERS June

SCENTED No

ASPECT South, east or west facing, in a sheltered position, with protection from cold or drying winds; full sun to partial shade

SOIL Any fertile, humus-rich, reliably moist, boggy soil

HARDINESS Fully hardy/borderline at temperatures down to -15°C/5°F; may need winter protection in colder areas

DROUGHT TOLERANCE Beyond poor

PROBLEMS Slugs and snails

CARE Mulch with organic matter in spring; cut back dying leaves in autumn; dry mulch crowns in winter

PROPAGATION Division in spring, before crown growth starts

Iris 'Dusky Challenger' (TB)

⬆ 1.2m/4ft ⬌ 1.2m/4ft **EASY**

Bearded irises are valued for the sumptuous elegance of their flowers, available in a huge colour assortment and a range of sizes. This hardy rhizomatous perennial has erect, sword-like pale green leaves and tall, smooth, sturdy stems, each topped with multiple flower buds, opening to reveal shamelessly extravagant silk-ruffled, deep rich purple, fragrant flowers with matching brooding, purple beards or 'falls'. *I.* 'Ice Dancer' (TB) ♛ has pale blue flowers, tinted white; *I.* 'Skyfire' (TB) has tangerine orange flowers; both are smaller, at 90cm/3ft.

BEST USES Fabulous in formal beds and borders; quite exceptional in a hot-coloured border or gravel garden; ideal for coastal gardens

FLOWERS May to June

SCENTED Scented flowers

ASPECT South or west facing, in a sheltered position; full sun

SOIL Any fertile, moist, well-drained soil

HARDINESS Fully hardy at temperatures down to -15°C/5°F; needs no winter protection

DROUGHT TOLERANCE Poor

PROBLEMS Slugs and snails

CARE Remove about a third of the top leaves after planting to help plant establish; cut back after flowering; mulch with organic matter annually in spring

PROPAGATION Division in autumn

Kirengeshoma palmata ⚇

⬆ 1.2m/4ft ⬌ 90cm/3ft   **EASY**

This is an architectural, clump-forming Japanese perennial with smooth, arching, wiry, wine-coloured stems and handsome sycamore-like deep green leaves, topped with small, waxy, pendent, bell-shaped, pale to bright yellow flowers. It deserves to be more popular as it is a lovely plant for bringing interest into shady gardens late in the season. There are no other varieties worth mentioning.

BEST USES This plant is most at home in acidic, shady woodland, where its mounded, multi-layered leafy hummocks make excellent ground cover; it will grace a flower border as long as you have the space and the right soil

FLOWERS August to September

SCENTED No

ASPECT North, east or west facing, in a sheltered position, with protection from strong winds; partial to full shade

SOIL Any fertile, moist, well-drained acid (lime-free) soil

HARDINESS Fully hardy at temperatures down to -15°C/5°F; needs no winter protection

DROUGHT TOLERANCE Poor

PROBLEMS Slugs and snails

CARE Mulch with organic matter annually in spring to help retain moisture at the roots; cut back spent flowering stems in late autumn

PROPAGATION Division in spring

Lilium 'Miss Lucy'

⬆ 1.2m/4ft ⬌ 60cm/24in   **EASY**

This Asian bulbous perennial carries my moniker and, since I don't have a plant named after me, I have adopted this one. An Oriental variety, it has a stiff, upright habit with sparse, glossy, lance-shaped mid-green leaves and is stamen free (so no pollen stains). The short, branched stems bear showy, gorgeously fragrant, large, double, trumpet flowers, white flushed with palest pink. Two new cultivars are L. 'Mambo' (90cm/3ft), with deep red flowers, and L. 'Tiger Woods' (90cm/3ft), with fragrant, rose-white flowers, striped pink, with plum speckles.

BEST USES An elegant addition to the summer or cottage garden border; attractive to pollinating insects; does well in pots; excellent as cut flowers

FLOWERS July to August

SCENTED Yes

ASPECT South, east or west facing, in a sheltered position; full sun

SOIL Any fertile, humus-rich, moisture-retentive soil; prefers acid soils or peat-free soil in containers

HARDINESS Fully hardy/borderline at temperatures down to -15°C/5°F; may need winter protection in colder areas

DROUGHT TOLERANCE Poor

PROBLEMS Aphids, scarlet lily beetle, slugs, snails and vine weevil; Botrytis (grey mould)

CARE Cut back spent flower stems

PROPAGATION Division in autumn or early spring; pot up bulblets in summer

Lychnis × arkwrightii 'Vesuvius'
Campion

⬆ 1.2m/4ft ↔ 30cm/12in   **EASY**

Found in alpine regions, woods and meadows across the northern hemisphere, lychnis are erect perennials with flowers that are usually red or pink and can be tubular or star or saucer-shaped. They are traditional cottage garden favourites, but there are also smaller alpines, more suited to raised beds or rock gardens. This hybrid is a short-lived perennial that is easy to care for, forming a fairly stiff, upright clump of bristly, oval, chocolate-bronze leaves, below tall stems that have branching, single, star-shaped, gappy, warm burnt orange flowers.

BEST USES Excellent for the wildflower or cottage garden (and it is loved by bees and butterflies); terrific for a hot-coloured or exotic border, or planted with ornamental grasses; lasts well as a cut flower

FLOWERS June to August
SCENTED No
ASPECT South, east or west facing, in a sheltered position; full sun to partial shade
SOIL Any fertile, well-drained soil
HARDINESS Fully hardy at temperatures down to -15°C/5°F; needs no winter protection
DROUGHT TOLERANCE Good, once established
PROBLEMS Aphids, slugs and snails
CARE May need staking; cut back flower stems after flowering
PROPAGATION Self-seeds easily, producing similar plants; division in spring

Lythrum salicaria 'Feuerkerze' (syn. L.s. Firecandle) ⚕ Purple loosestrife

⬆ 1.5m/5ft ↔ 45cm/18in   **EASY**

Originating in riversides and ditches across Europe and Asia, this tall, clump-forming perennial for damp places has dark green, lance-shaped leaves and bears tall, straight stems with striking, slender sky rockets of double, starry magenta-pink flowers, densely studded along the stalks. L.s. 'Feuerkerze' is sterile, but other varieties self-seed prolifically and can become invasive. Other worthy contenders are paler pink L.s. 'Blush' (1.2m/4ft) and L.s. 'Robert' ⚕ (1.5m/5ft) with pinky mauve flowers.

BEST USES The tall, colourful flowers are perfect at the back of an informal border; a great lure for bees and butterflies in a wildflower garden; ideal for coastal gardens

FLOWERS July to September
SCENTED No
ASPECT South or west facing, in a sheltered or exposed position; full sun
SOIL Any fertile, moist or boggy, waterlogged soil; loves heavy clay
HARDINESS Fully hardy at temperatures down to -15°C/5°F; needs no winter protection
DROUGHT TOLERANCE Poor
PROBLEMS Slugs and snails love young shoots
CARE Remove spent flower stems to prevent energetic self-seeding; cut down to just above ground level in autumn
PROPAGATION Division in spring; basal stem cuttings in spring to early summer

Macleaya microcarpa 'Kelway's Coral Plume' 🏅 Plume poppy

⬆ 2.5m/8ft ⬌ 90cm/3ft   **EASY**

This sizeable clump-forming rhizomatous perennial of Asian origin is grown for its large, ornamental, scalloped olive green leaves (20cm/8in wide), felty white underneath, and tall, erect stems that produce plumed clouds of tiny pink or creamy beige flowers (60cm/24in long) in mid-summer. It is a lovely diaphanous plant requiring plenty of space, but seldom needs staking. Other species with similar foliage and flowers are *M. cordata* 🏅 (biscuit-coloured flowers) and *M. × kewensis* 'Flamingo' 🏅 (pale pink flowers), both 2.5m/8ft tall. All tend to be invasive, especially on light, sandy soils.

BEST USES Wonderful naturalised with tall grasses in the prairie or wildflower garden; a showy plant with *Verbena bonariensis* and tall poppies

FLOWERS June to July
SCENTED No
ASPECT South, east or west facing, in a sheltered position, with protection from cold winds; full sun to partial shade
SOIL Any fertile, moist, well-drained soil
HARDINESS Frost hardy, at temperatures down to -5°C/23°F; needs winter protection
DROUGHT TOLERANCE Poor
PROBLEMS Slugs and snails may nibble young growth
CARE Cut back to just above ground level in autumn; dry mulch in winter
PROPAGATION Division in late autumn or spring; root cuttings in winter

Meconopsis betonicifolia 🏅
Tibetan blue poppy

⬆ 1.2m/4ft ⬌ 45cm/18in   **TRICKY**

This clump-forming Tibetan perennial is short-lived and difficult to establish, but you will be the envy of everyone if you can get it going. It has bristly, toothed, heart-shaped, blue-hued green leaves at the base. In early summer, tall, upright bristly stems are topped with clusters of sky blue salver-shaped flowers, with yellow eyes and stamens. It flowers so briefly that it is an extravagance, but what a luxury!

BEST USES Ideal in a woodland garden (where other plants distract from the shortness of its visit)

FLOWERS June
SCENTED No
ASPECT South or west facing, in a sheltered position, with protection from winds; partial shade
SOIL Any fertile, moist, well-drained soil; prefers slight acidity; avoid winter wet, which causes it to rot
HARDINESS Fully hardy at temperatures down to -15°C/5°F; needs no winter protection
DROUGHT TOLERANCE Poor
PROBLEMS Slugs and snails; powdery mildew
CARE Mulch with organic matter annually in spring; needs staking; don't let it flower in the first year; remove spent flower spikes to prolong flowering
PROPAGATION Division after flowering; sow ripe seed immediately in pots in a cold frame (use loamless compost) (P.S. I've tried and failed)

GREENFINGER TIP *If it fails to flower, you will notice that several crowns grow, giving you a second chance*

Rheum palmatum var. tanguticum
Chinese rhubarb

↑ 2m/6ft ↔ 2m/6ft   **EASY**

This architectural rhizomatous perennial from China is a whopper, with thick, rhubarby stems and large, torpedo-like, shiny red buds that open in spring to bear huge, very ornamental, veined, toothed, deep purple leaves, flushed purple-bronze underneath, some 90cm/3ft across. In summer, it bears tall livid wands of tiny rosy red flowers, clustered in large conical plumes, up to 2m/6ft high. *R.p.* 'Bowles's Crimson' has deeply veined green leaves, crimson underneath, from June to August.

BEST USES Adds drama as a long-lived focal point in any border; ideal for a shady border or in wet, boggy soil near a stream or pond edge; the exotic foliage looks good in a 'hot' border; insects love it

FLOWERS June to July
SCENTED No
ASPECT South, east or west facing, in a sheltered position; full sun to partial shade
SOIL Any fertile, humus-rich, moisture-retentive soil
HARDINESS Fully hardy at temperatures down to -15°C/5°F; needs no winter protection
DROUGHT TOLERANCE Poor
PROBLEMS Slugs and snails; crown rot
CARE Mulch with organic matter annually in spring
PROPAGATION Division in spring; sow seed in pots in a cold frame in autumn

GREENFINGER TIP *If you lack the space for a gunnera, this makes a worthy substitute*

Rodgersia pinnata 'Superba' ♟

↑ 1.5m/5ft ↔ 90cm/3ft   **EASY**

Rodgersias are clump-forming rhizomatous herbaceous perennials from China, much coveted for their handsome foliage of large palmate leaves (20cm/8in across), appealingly flushed bronze-purple. In summer, they send up slender, branching reddish stems topped with tiny, star-shaped flowers that form soft plumes of rosy pink flowers, some 50cm/20in tall, on straight, smooth, red-brown stems. Every garden needs large-foliaged plants to set off more delicate planting or a border can look very bitty. *R.p.* 'Chocolate Wing' (60cm/24in tall) has gorgeous chocolate-burgundy leaves.

BEST USES Makes a strong impact in a cottage garden or formal flower border; tolerant of dappled shade, so ideal for a shady border; useful in a wild garden by a stream or pond edge as insects love it

FLOWERS July to August
SCENTED No
ASPECT South, east or west facing, in a sheltered position; full sun to partial shade
SOIL Any fertile, humus-rich, moisture-retentive, well-drained soil
HARDINESS Fully hardy at temperatures down to -15°C/5°F; needs no winter protection
DROUGHT TOLERANCE Poor
PROBLEMS Slugs and snails like to nibble young foliage
CARE Mulch with organic matter annually in spring; cut back spent flowering stems
PROPAGATION Division in spring

Verbascum (Cotswold Group) 'Gainsborough' ♀ Mullein

⬆ 1.2m/4ft ⬌ 30cm/12in   **EASY**

Originating in dry stony terrain in Africa, central Asia and Europe, this statuesque, semi-evergreen perennial has crinkled, felted, grey-green oval leaves that are arranged rosette fashion, from which arise tall, woolly flower stems, studded along their length with flower buds that open to reveal shallow, cupped pale yellow flowers from early summer. All self-seed freely. *V.* (C.G.) 'Cotswold Queen' has buff-orange flowers; *V.* (C.G.) 'Pink Domino' ♀ has rose pink flowers; both are1.2m/4ft tall.

BEST USES Leave to self-seed for vertical accents through a gravel garden or Mediterranean border; very attractive to pollinating insects

FLOWERS June to August
SCENTED No
ASPECT South or west facing, in a sheltered or exposed position; full sun
SOIL Any poor to moderately fertile, well-drained soil; avoid very waterlogged soil
HARDINESS Fully hardy at temperatures down to -15°C/5°F; needs no winter protection
DROUGHT TOLERANCE Excellent, once established (particularly self-sown seedlings)
PROBLEMS Powdery mildew
CARE Remove spent flowers to curb self-seeding; cut back to just above ground level in late winter or spring
PROPAGATION Self-seeds easily; sow seed in pots in a cold frame in spring or early summer; root cuttings in winter

Veronicastrum virginicum 'Album' Culver's root

⬆ 1.2m/4ft ⬌ 45cm/18in   **EASY**

This tall, upright North American perennial has narrow, whorled, serrated dark green leaves and bears profuse, gauzy, tapering spires comprising myriad tiny white tubular flowers in late summer. It is a much under-rated plant that is undemanding and rarely needs staking. *V.v.* 'Erica' (1.2m/4ft) has pinky red flowers with red foliage; *V.v.* 'Fascination' (1.5m/5ft) has lavender flowers tipped with coral stamens; *V.v.* f. *roseum* (1.5m/5ft) has soft pink flowers.

BEST USES Ideal in a large informal border; plant swathes at intervals to knit a wildflower or prairie garden together and add rhythm to the planting scheme; bees and butterflies adore it

FLOWERS July to August
SCENTED No
ASPECT Any, in a sheltered or exposed position; full sun to partial shade
SOIL Any fertile, moist, humus-rich soil
HARDINESS Fully hardy at temperatures down to -15°C/5°F; needs no winter protection
DROUGHT TOLERANCE Poor
PROBLEMS Leaf spot and powdery mildew
CARE Water generously at the roots to avoid powdery mildew, especially in dry weather
PROPAGATION Division in spring; sow seed in pots in a cold frame in autumn

AUTUMN

Warm evenings, scented with wood smoke and the dying embers of the barbecue season, bring autumn-flowering border plants into a mellow arena of their own. Soft golds, rich reds, deep burgundies and burnt oranges herald the arrival of autumn days and the garden becomes a more chilled, tranquil space. There is a wide choice of autumn-flowering plants, from the diminutive to the statuesque, that will keep your garden flowering long after the hazy days of summer have passed and they are all the more alluring for their late but significant arrival.

Agastache 'Blue Fortune' 🎖
Mexican giant hyssop

⬆ 60cm/24in ⬌ 30cm/12in   EASY

Hyssops are short-lived half-hardy perennials found in dry, hilly areas from Asia and the USA to Mexico, so thrive on poor, hungry soils. This bushy, clump-forming herbaceous perennial has liquorice-scented, lance-shaped, pointed deep green leaves (resembling mint leaves) that make dense leafy mounds and tall, straight green stems with strong, upright flower spikes, comprising myriad tiny blue tubular flowers. Agastaches generally flower in summer, but this variety continues producing flowers well into autumn and is irresistible to bees and butterflies. *A.* 'Black Adder' (90cm/3ft) is taller and has deeper violet flowers.

BEST USES Ideal for a Mediterranean or gravel garden; being such a lure to bees, it does well in the cottage and wildflower garden too

FLOWERS July to October
SCENTED Aromatic leaves
ASPECT South or west facing, in a sheltered position; full sun
SOIL Any fertile, well-drained soil
HARDINESS Frost hardy at temperatures down to -5°C/23°F; needs winter protection
DROUGHT TOLERANCE Good, once established
PROBLEMS Powdery mildew
CARE Cut back faded flowers in late winter or early spring
PROPAGATION Division in spring

Chrysanthemum 'Ruby Mound' 🎖

⬆ 30cm/12in ⬌ 60cm/24in   MEDIUM

These autumn-flowering hardy perennials from Asia come in a bewildering range of colours and flower shape (pompon, single or double) and tend to be smaller than the less hardy summer-flowering chrysanthemums. This compact, slightly woody-based, bushy, clump-forming variety sends up straight, dense leafy stems with toothed green leaves and sprays of double flowers of deep, rich brick red flowers. Other compact varieties include burnt orange C. 'Paul Boissier' and single, vivid pink C. 'Venus One'.

BEST USES Invaluable for late colour in the border; try them at the front of the border or in pots, plunged into the border or in a sunny spot on a city patio

FLOWERS October to November

SCENTED No

ASPECT South or west facing, in a sheltered position; full sun

SOIL Any fertile, well-drained soil

HARDINESS Fully hardy at temperatures down to -15°C/5°F; needs no winter protection

DROUGHT TOLERANCE Poor

PROBLEMS Aphids, capsid bug, earwigs, eelworms and leaf miners; *Botrytis* (grey mould) and powdery mildew

CARE Cut back after flowering; dry mulch crowns in cold areas

PROPAGATION Division in early spring every three years, as new growth appears; basal stem cuttings in spring

Commelina tuberosa Coelestis Group
Widow's tears

⬆ 45cm/18in ⬌ 30cm/12in   MEDIUM

This clump-forming, tuberous, frost-hardy perennial (often grown as an annual) comes from Central and South America and is a new plant to me, covetously espied growing in a friend's garden, where it formed a generous, somewhat upright clump of vivid, fresh green, oblongish leaves. It was smothered in small, three-petalled sky blue flowers with yellow stamens, held on fleshy, lightly hairy stems with black markings at intervals along their length. *C.t.* 'Alba' has white flowers.

BEST USES Makes colourful leafy hummocks in a cottage garden or at the front of an informal border; does well in containers in a city garden; bees love it, so a good choice for the wildflower garden

FLOWERS July to October

SCENTED No

ASPECT South or west, in a sheltered position; full sun to partial shade

SOIL Any fertile, well-drained soil

HARDINESS Frost hardy at temperatures down to -5°C/23°F; needs winter protection

DROUGHT TOLERANCE Good, once established

PROBLEMS Slugs, snails and vine weevil

CARE Dry mulch the crown in winter; in cold regions, lift tubers out of the ground and replant in late spring when all risk of frost has passed

PROPAGATION Self-seeds easily; division in spring

Cyclamen hederifolium ⚕

⬆ 10–13cm/4–5in ⬌ 15cm/6in   **MEDIUM**

This tuberous Mediterranean perennial has ivy-like, heart-shaped green leaves, marbled with cream, that make rounded glossy clumps, and produces scented, upright, butterfly-like deep pink flowers, flushed plum at the base, that are 2.5cm/1in long, carried on smooth, slender, short, reddish stems from mid-autumn. The leaves usually appear after the flowers, and look good from autumn through to spring, when they die back down. *C.h.* var. *hederifolium* f. *albiflorum* (10cm/4in) is the white-flowered variety.

> **BEST USES** Ideal as a woodland plant and under trees, where little else will grow; marvellous as ground cover in a shady shrubbery; will also take a sunny position at the front of a border

FLOWERS October to January
SCENTED Yes
ASPECT Any, in a sheltered position; full sun to partial shade
SOIL Any humus-rich, moist, well-drained soil; dislikes sitting in wet
HARDINESS Fully hardy at temperatures down to -15°C/5°F; needs no winter protection
DROUGHT TOLERANCE Poor
PROBLEMS Vine weevil; mice and squirrels
CARE Dry mulch crowns in spring in frost-prone areas
PROPAGATION Self-seeds reasonably well; sow ripe seed in July in a dark place, excluding daylight, at 6–12°C/43–54°F

Erigeron karvinskianus ⚕
Mexican fleabane/Spanish daisy

⬆ 20cm/8in ⬌ 60cm/24in   **EASY**

This Mexican spreading perennial has a lax habit with small, ferny, lance-shaped green leaves. It bears an extravagant profusion of small daisy-like flowers that have white petals, flushed pink, with cheerful yellow centres, and is one of the handiest plants I know because of its ability to survive all weathers. The long flowering period is a real bonus: although it flowers earlier in the year, I have seen it going right into November in milder areas.

> **BEST USES** A cheerful plant that happily fills gaps at the front of a border or will tumble down walls, cover dry banks and pop up between paving and in drystone walls; does well underplanting larger specimens in containers

FLOWERS June to October, often until first frosts
SCENTED No
ASPECT South, east or west facing, in a sheltered position; full sun
SOIL Any fertile, well-drained soil
HARDINESS Fully hardy at temperatures down to -15°C/5°F; needs no winter protection
DROUGHT TOLERANCE Excellent, once established
PROBLEMS None
CARE Trim back lightly in spring (hard if unruly); cut back after flowering to limit self-seeding
PROPAGATION Self-seeds easily; division in early spring

Geranium × oxonianum 'Wargrave Pink' ⚕ Cranesbill

⬆ 60cm/24in ⬌ 90cm/3ft   **EASY**

This hardy herbaceous perennial hybrid is one of the more vigorous geraniums and its evergreen scalloped mid-green leaves are quick to clump up. Short, slender stems hold an absolute multitude of simple, saucer-shaped, five-petalled, prettily veined, shell pink flowers from late spring to early autumn, making it value for money in the flowering department. *G. × o.* 'A.T. Johnson' ⚕ (30cm/12in) is more compact, with silvery pink flowers; *G. × o.* 'Hollywood' (45cm/18in) has pale pink flowers with dark claret veining.

BEST USES Ideal in the cottage garden or repeated through a large formal flower bed to give unity to a planting scheme; a great plant for underplanting in a mixed border; makes fantastic ground cover

FLOWERS May to October

SCENTED No

ASPECT Any, in a sheltered or exposed position; full sun to partial shade

SOIL Any fertile, moist, well-drained soil

HARDINESS Fully hardy at temperatures down to -15°C/5°F; needs no winter protection

DROUGHT TOLERANCE Poor

PROBLEMS Downy and powdery mildew

CARE Cut back faded flowers and tatty leaves to encourage new growth and more flowers; cut back hard in spring

PROPAGATION Division in spring

Liriope muscari ⚕
Lily turf

⬆ 30cm/12in ⬌ 45cm/18in   **EASY**

This ever-popular, Chinese, clump-forming, tuberous evergreen perennial has bright green leaves in grass-like blades and produces masses of sturdy, short, purplish pillars, smothered in tiny, purple-blue flowers that look very much like grape hyacinths, in late summer to autumn. Small black berries follow the flowers. They soon form natural-looking colonies of vivid colour if left undisturbed and are pretty unfussy about soil and site. *L.m.* 'Gold-banded' has golden-edged leaves; *L.m.* 'Okina' has bleached white leaves and purple flowers; and *L.m.* 'Royal Purple' has deep purple flowers.

BEST USES Grow at the front of a border; naturalise in grassland or woodland; makes effective ground cover in light shade under shrubs; looks pretty in containers

FLOWERS August to November

SCENTED No

ASPECT Any, in a sheltered position, with protection from cold winds; full sun to full shade

SOIL Any fertile, moist, well-drained soil

HARDINESS Fully hardy at temperatures down to -15°C/5°F; needs no winter protection

DROUGHT TOLERANCE Good, once established

PROBLEMS Slugs and snails

CARE Mulch with organic matter annually in spring; cut back old tatty foliage in spring

PROPAGATION Division in spring to early summer; sow seed in spring in pots outdoors

Nerine bowdenii 🏆
Nerine

⬆ 45cm/18in ⬌ 10cm/4in   **MEDIUM**

It is no wonder this bulbous South African perennial is a popular choice for the autumn flower border. It has fresh green, strappy leaves from late winter, but these die back in summer, and in autumn the tall bare stems suddenly produce large musky-scented, pretty, spidery, trumpet-shaped bubble-gum pink flowers that are startlingly exotic against tawny autumn colours. *N.b.* f. *alba* has white flowers.

> **BEST USES** Grows well in containers; the colour effect is fantastic when planted in a good strong block in a border; excellent as cut flowers

FLOWERS September to November

SCENTED Scented flowers

ASPECT South, east or west facing; full sun

SOIL Any reasonable, well-drained soil; does well in poor, dry soils

HARDINESS Fully hardy at temperatures down to -15°C/5°F; needs no winter protection

DROUGHT TOLERANCE Excellent, once established

PROBLEMS Slugs and snails

CARE Plant bulbs in early spring, with the tips just visible above the soil; water with a low-nitrogen feed after flowering; dry mulch with straw in winter in cold areas

PROPAGATION Division in spring; sow ripe seed immediately at 10–13°C/50–55°F

....

GREENFINGER TIP *Don't worry if, over time, the bulbs break the soil surface and appear congested: they like their feet cramped and baking hot*

Physostegia virginiana 'Summer Snow' 🏆
Obedient plant

⬆ 60cm/24in ⬌ 60cm/24in   **EASY**

This North American erect rhizomatous perennial is a graceful plant, with fresh, toothed leaves and double-lipped, pure white tubular flowers with green calyces, carried in plenty on smooth, straight, squarish, branched stems. They open from the bottom up, from late summer into autumn. *P.v.* var. *speciosa* 'Variegata' has pale pink flowers with green leaves edged pink and cream; *P.v.* 'Vivid' 🏆 has rosy pink flowers.

> **BEST USES** Ideal for any flower border; does well in pots if the compost is kept moist; brightens up a damp (but not waterlogged) shady corner

FLOWERS August to October

SCENTED No

ASPECT South, east or west facing, in a sheltered position; full sun to partial shade

SOIL Any fertile, moist, well-drained soil

HARDINESS Fully hardy at temperatures down to -15°C/5°F; needs no winter protection

DROUGHT TOLERANCE Poor

PROBLEMS Slugs and snails

CARE Mulch with organic matter annually in spring; cut down to just above ground level in winter

PROPAGATION Division before new growth starts in winter to early spring; sow seed in pots in a cold frame in autumn

....

GREENFINGER TIP *This is called the obedient plant because the flowers don't spring back when moved on the stems but stay in their new position*

Schizostylis coccinea 'Jennifer' ♗
Kaffir lily

⬆ 60cm/24in ⬌ 30cm/12in   **MEDIUM**

These clump-forming, rhizomatous perennials come from South Africa and flower from late summer to early winter, providing an exotic, colourful addition to the fading garden tapestry. This variety has bright green, narrow, linear, grassy leaves and slender stems, carrying delicate, open, cupped flowers that are pale shell pink, flushed white inside (5–6cm/2–2½in long). *S.c.* f. *alba* is white-flowered; *S.c.* 'Major' ♗ is a bulkier plant than other varieties, worth investigating for its bold, bright red flowers.

BEST USES Ideal by ponds or streams; good in borders or containers; excellent as cut flowers to brighten the winter table

FLOWERS August to November
SCENTED No
ASPECT South or west facing, in a sheltered position; full sun
SOIL Any fertile, moist, well-drained soil
HARDINESS Frost hardy at temperatures down to -10°C/14°F; frosts can damage the flowers
DROUGHT TOLERANCE Poor
PROBLEMS Frost
CARE Deadhead and remove stems after flowering, raking away dead foliage; mulch with organic matter annually in spring; don't let the roots dry out during the growing season (they like reliably moist soil)
PROPAGATION Division in spring

Sedum telephium Atropurpureum Group ♗ Ice plant

⬆ 60cm/24in ⬌ 30cm/12in   **EASY**

The tall sedums are upright, clump-forming, succulent perennials, found from Asia to Europe, that come into their own in autumn. This stunning example has fleshy, pointed, oval, damson-coloured leaves and short, smooth, branching, moody purple stems, topped with domed flower heads. These are made up of tiny rounded buds that open to tiny star-shaped blooms, massed together to form the pink domes (some 13cm/5in across) in late summer, fading to beige in autumn. *S.t.* Atropurpureum Group 'Purple Emperor' ♗ (45cm/18in) has red-purple flower heads and red-bronze foliage.

BEST USES Perfect for a dry, parched spot in a sunny border; provides colour and sculptural form in the late border; bees and butterflies adore it

FLOWERS July to October
SCENTED No
ASPECT South or west facing, in a sheltered position; full sun
SOIL Any fertile, well-drained soil
HARDINESS Fully hardy at temperatures down to -15°C/5°F; needs no winter protection
DROUGHT TOLERANCE Excellent, once established
PROBLEMS Slugs, snails and vine weevil
CARE Mulch with organic matter annually in spring; may need staking, as the flower heads are heavy; remove spent flower heads or leave them for winter interest
PROPAGATION Self-seeds easily; division in spring

Silene schafta
Autumn catchfly

25cm/10in ⟷ 30cm/12in — EASY

This diminutive semi-evergreen alpine perennial, from Asia, is incredibly useful for its vivid flowering from late summer well into autumn. It forms pleasing low mounds of bright green, small pointed leaves and bears a profusion of tubular, gappy, starry, vibrant magenta flowers. *S.s.* 'Shell Pink' has pale shell pink flowers.

BEST USES A good edging plant for the front of the border; excellent ground cover for slopes and rockeries; does well in containers

FLOWERS August to October
SCENTED No
ASPECT South, east or west facing, in a sheltered or exposed position; full sun to partial shade
SOIL Any fertile, well-drained soil; dislikes sitting in winter wet
HARDINESS Fully hardy at temperatures down to -15°C/5°F; needs no winter protection
DROUGHT TOLERANCE Poor
PROBLEMS Downy and powdery mildew
CARE Deadhead after flowering to encourage compact, dense growth
PROPAGATION Sow seed in pots in a cold frame in autumn

Tradescantia Andersoniana Group 'Zwanenburg Blue' **Spider lily**

60cm/24in ⟷ 50cm/20in — EASY

Gardeners often overlook the merits of these evergreen, clump-forming perennials from the Americas. Their narrow, strappy, pointed blades of foliage provide a perfect foil for the clusters of tri-lobed flowers that nestle appealingly in the leaf axils. They are easy to grow and flower reliably from summer to autumn. This charming variety has slightly fleshy, arching, linear green leaves and striking royal blue flowers with golden stamens. *T.* Andersoniana Group 'Sweet Kate' (50cm/20in) has golden foliage with bright blue flowers; *T.A.G.* 'Isis' has violet flowers.

BEST USES Excellent for formal borders or raised beds; ideal at the front of a cottage garden border; a definite lure for bees and insects

FLOWERS June to October
SCENTED No
ASPECT South, east or west facing, in a sheltered position; full sun to partial shade
SOIL Any fertile, humus-rich, moisture-retentive soil
HARDINESS Fully hardy at temperatures down to -15°C/5°F; needs no winter protection
DROUGHT TOLERANCE Poor
PROBLEMS Leaves may scorch in full sun
CARE Stake to avoid flopping in wet weather; cut stems back to the base after flowering
PROPAGATION Division in autumn or spring

GREENFINGER TIP *They can produce too much foliage and become congested, so division may be a necessity*

Anaphalis triplinervis 'Sommerschnee' ♟
Pearl everlasting

⬆ 70cm/28in ⬌ 45–60cm/18–24in   **EASY**

This clump-forming, bushy, herbaceous perennial from Asia has narrow, silver green-grey, hairy foliage with white felty undersides. The stiff, upright stems bear sprays of domed clusters of tiny, rounded, bobble-like, long-lasting papery flowers that are pure white with yellow centres and last well into autumn.

> **BEST USES** An adaptable plant, bringing long flowering interest and silver foliage into any flower border; especially good for white or seaside gardens; popular for dried flower arrangements

FLOWERS July to October

SCENTED No

ASPECT Any, in a sheltered or exposed position; full sun to partial shade

SOIL Any fertile, moist, well-drained soil

HARDINESS Fully hardy at temperatures down to -15°C/5°F; needs no winter protection

DROUGHT TOLERANCE Poor

PROBLEMS None

CARE Cut back hard after flowering to encourage further flowering and keep the plant bushy

PROPAGATION Division in spring; sow seed in pots in a cold frame in spring

Aster × frikartii 'Mönch' ♟
Michaelmas daisy

⬆ 90cm/3ft ⬌ 60cm/24in   **EASY**

Michaelmas daisies are a huge group, including annuals and rockery plants as well as perennials, in a range of colours from reds to blues, purples, pinks and white, and are invaluable for bringing late colour into borders. This bushy herbaceous perennial from the Himalayas has an upright habit with matt, narrow, lance-shaped deep green leaves and masses of branching sprays of lavender blue flowers with daisy-like petals, radiating from orange-brown centres, followed by fluffy seed heads. Happily, this hybrid doesn't suffer much from the aster weakness of powdery mildew. *A. × f.* 'Flora's Delight' has pale lilac flowers.

> **BEST USES** A cottage garden favourite; ideal for beds and borders or growing in containers (plunge the pots into gaps in the late summer border); excellent as cut flowers

FLOWERS August to October

SCENTED No

ASPECT Any, in a sheltered or exposed position; full sun to partial shade

SOIL Any fertile, moist, well-drained soil

HARDINESS Fully hardy at temperatures down to -15°C/5°F; needs no winter protection

DROUGHT TOLERANCE Good, once established

PROBLEMS Powdery mildew, though this variety has good resistance

CARE Mulch with organic matter annually in spring; may need staking

PROPAGATION Division in spring

Dahlia 'Bishop of Llandaff' ♛
Dahlia

↑ 90cm/3ft ↔ 45cm/18in   MEDIUM

Dahlias are upright tuberous perennials of Mexican origin. This famed, peony-like border dahlia is much in vogue for its vivid deep red semi-double flowers, marked with a chocolate brown eye, fringed with golden stamens. It has handsome, deeply dissected green to purple-black foliage. Other notable border dahlias include D. 'Jescot Julie', with bright orange flowers, and D. 'Moonfire' ♛ (75cm/30in), with apricot, flushed orange, blooms.

BEST USES Perfect to extend the life of hot coloured borders in autumn with bold tones

FLOWERS July to October
SCENTED No
ASPECT South or west facing, in a sheltered position; full sun
SOIL Any fertile, humus-rich, well-drained soil
HARDINESS Half hardy, withstanding temperatures down to 0°C/32°F; needs protection from winter cold and frosts
DROUGHT TOLERANCE Poor
PROBLEMS Aphids, capsid bug, caterpillars, earwigs, slugs and snails
CARE Needs staking; deadhead to prolong flowering; feed with a high nitrogen feed weekly in June; in warm areas, cover tubers with a dry mulch in winter (in colder areas, lift tubers once foliage has blackened, store in a frost-free place over winter and replant once risk of frost has passed)
PROPAGATION Division of shooting tubers

Gaillardia × grandiflora 'Dazzler' ♛
Blanket flower

↑ 90cm/3ft ↔ 50cm/20in   EASY

Found in sunny, open spaces in North and South America, this extrovert clump-forming herbaceous perennial is short-lived but can also be grown as an annual. It has long, narrow, pointed grey-green leaves on slightly bristly straight stems and bears a profusion of large, flat, daisy-like deep orange flowers (7–14cm/3–5in across), flaring to golden yellow tips, in summer and autumn. G. × g. 'Burgunder' (60cm/24in) has large maroon flowers.

BEST USES Provides a burst of cheerful colour in the exotic or cottage garden autumn border; ideal for wildflower gardens as pollinating insects love them; does well in coastal areas

FLOWERS June to October
SCENTED No
ASPECT South or west facing, in a sheltered position; full sun
SOIL Any fertile, well-drained soil
HARDINESS Fully hardy at temperatures down to -15°C/5°F; needs no winter protection
DROUGHT TOLERANCE Good, once established
PROBLEMS Powdery mildew
CARE Deadhead regularly and cut back after flowering has finished
PROPAGATION Sow seed in seed trays or pots at 18–25°C/64–77°F in a greenhouse in spring to early summer

Helenium 'Autumn Lollipop'

⬆ 90m/3ft ⬌ 60cm/24in   EASY

Heleniums are South American herbaceous perennials and their vibrant red, yellow and coppery orange flowers (usually daisy-like, often rayed) add reliable late colour to the border. This architectural, clump-forming variety has large, toothed, bright green leaves and tall, straight, slightly bristly stems topped with unusual golden yellow flowers that look like drumsticks, with large red-brown centres, fringed with yellow eyelashes at their base.

BEST USES Great for sustaining colour in the late-summer flower border; adapts well to prairie-style planting; bees and other insects adore it

FLOWERS August to October

SCENTED No

ASPECT South, east or west facing, in a sheltered or exposed position; full sun

SOIL Any fertile, moist, humus-rich, well-drained soil

HARDINESS Fully hardy at temperatures down to -15°C/5°F; needs no winter protection

DROUGHT TOLERANCE Poor

PROBLEMS Leaf spot

CARE May need staking; deadhead to stimulate flowers; divide every 2–3 years to keep vigorous

PROPAGATION Division in autumn or spring; basal stem cuttings in spring

GREENFINGER TIP *If the plant is growing too tall, pinch out the growing tips around June so it will be shorter when it flowers*

Inula hookeri

⬆ 90cm/3ft ⬌ 60cm/24in   EASY

Inula is a joyful addition to the autumn border. A clump-forming herbaceous perennial from the Himalayas, it is extremely robust, making large, spreading clumps in no time. It has tall, hairy stems, softly bristly, lightly toothed, oval green leaves and a frenzied profusion of shaggy, starburst, daisy-like pale yellow flowers, with pale golden brown centres, from late summer well into autumn. Often you can barely see the flowers as they are smothered in bees.

BEST USES Does well in woodland, cottage or coastal gardens; pollinating insects love it so it is good for the wildflower garden; self-seeds prolifically and you'll soon have thriving clumps

FLOWERS August to October

SCENTED No

ASPECT Any, in a sheltered or exposed position; partial shade

SOIL Any fertile, moist, well-drained soil

HARDINESS Fully hardy at temperatures down to -15°C/5°F; needs no winter protection

DROUGHT TOLERANCE Poor

PROBLEMS Powdery mildew

CARE Plants need staking; deadhead to prevent self-seeding

PROPAGATION Self-seeds easily; division in autumn or spring

Lobelia cardinalis ♀

⬆ 90cm/3ft ⬌ 30cm/12in   EASY

South American in origin, this is an invaluable (though short-lived) hardy perennial for late-summer and autumn borders. It's a clump-former with gorgeous narrow, pointed, bronze-burgundy foliage that sends up erect, self-supporting, purple flowering stems with tubular flowers that are a vibrant scarlet red; these open in succession from the bottom up. It is a knockout. *L.c.* 'Queen Victoria' ♀ has beetroot-coloured leaves and scarlet flowers.

BEST USES A stately plant for any late flower border and makes a bold change of pace from the mellow yellows of most autumn flowers; perfect for a hot-coloured, exotic border; great for butterflies and bees; excellent as a cut flower

FLOWERS July to October

SCENTED No

ASPECT South, east or west facing, in a sheltered position; full sun to partial shade

SOIL Any fertile, moist, well-drained soil

HARDINESS Fully hardy at temperatures down to -15°C/5°F; needs no winter protection

DROUGHT TOLERANCE Poor

PROBLEMS Slugs and snails

CARE Mulch with organic matter annually in spring; cut back spent flower spikes

PROPAGATION Division in spring; sow ripe seed immediately in pots in a cold frame

Penstemon 'Blackbird'

⬆ 75cm/30in ⬌ 45cm/18in   EASY

Originating from the north and central Americas, these evergreen or semi-evergreen perennials come in a glorious palette of colours and are a must for sustaining colour into late summer and autumn. This handsome, semi-evergreen clump-forming, bushy perennial, with lance-shaped green leaves, has tall, graceful burgundy stems, bearing deep damson tubular flowers, with contrasting white throats. Others include *P.* 'Alice Hindley' ♀ (pale mauve flowers), *P.* 'Apple Blossom' ♀ (pale pink), *P.* 'Flamingo' (pink and white) and *P.* 'Maurice Gibbs' ♀ (fuchsia pink with white throats).

BEST USES Plant at intervals through a formal or informal border to help establish continuity from summer to autumn

FLOWERS July to October

SCENTED No

ASPECT South, east or west facing, in a sheltered or exposed position; full sun to partial shade

SOIL Any fertile, well-drained soil

HARDINESS Fully hardy at temperatures down to -15°C/5°F; needs no winter protection

DROUGHT TOLERANCE Poor

PROBLEMS Eelworms, slugs and snails

CARE Mulch with organic matter annually in spring; cut back to just above ground level in spring; may need staking; deadhead spent flowers

PROPAGATION Division in spring; stem-tip cuttings in mid to late summer

Phlox paniculata 'Bright Eyes' ♉
Perennial phlox

⬆ 90cm/3ft ⬌ 60cm/24in   **EASY**

Phlox can be small, low-growing plants, but this is one of the taller border perennials, which originate in moist, riverside habitats in North America and are prized for their delicious perfume and varied hues. This bushy, upright herbaceous perennial has elliptical, divided leaves and tall, slim stems carrying domes of simple, sweetly scented shell pink flowers, flushed rosy red at the centres. *P.p.* 'Becky Towe' (60cm/24in) has variegated, gold-edged foliage and scented carmine flowers; *P.p.* 'David' (90cm/3ft) has fragrant, jasmine-like white flowers, and often flowers into early winter; *P.p.* 'Tenor' (90cm/3ft) has fragrant, rose pink flowers.

> **BEST USES** Indispensable low-maintenance plants for late-season colour; perfect in any flower border

FLOWERS July to October
SCENTED Yes
ASPECT South, east or west facing, in a sheltered or exposed position; full sun to partial shade
SOIL Any fertile, moist, well-drained soil
HARDINESS Fully hardy at temperatures down to -15°C/5°F; needs no winter protection
DROUGHT TOLERANCE Poor
PROBLEMS Eelworms; leaf spot and powdery mildew
CARE Mulch with organic matter in spring; may need staking; deadhead fading flowers to encourage new growth; cut down to just above ground level in winter
PROPAGATION Division in autumn or spring; sow seed in pots in a cold frame in spring

Rudbeckia fulgida var. sullivantii 'Goldsturm' ♉ Coneflower

⬆ 75cm/30in ⬌ 60cm/24in   **EASY**

Rudbeckias, from the USA, are enormously useful upright rhizomatous perennials, bringing warm colour into the late-summer and autumn garden. This is a short-stemmed species with the typical flat, golden yellow daisy-like flowers (9–12cm/3½–5½in across) that droop slightly, with very prominent brown-coned centres. The narrow, pointed, mid-green leaves have pronounced veining, but it is the profusion of flowers that commands attention. Golden yellow *R.f.* var. *deamii* ♉ tolerates partial shade.

> **BEST USES** Great for naturalising in a prairie planting scheme or wildflower garden (and insects love it); excellent for extending colour into autumn in formal or informal flower beds

FLOWERS August to October
SCENTED No
ASPECT South, east or west facing, in a sheltered or exposed position; full sun to partial shade
SOIL Any fertile, moist, well-drained soil
HARDINESS Fully hardy at temperatures down to -15°C/5°F; needs no winter protection
PROBLEMS Slugs and snails may nibble young foliage
DROUGHT TOLERANCE Poor
CARE Mulch with organic matter annually in spring; support plants with stakes
PROPAGATION Division in autumn or spring; sow seed in pots in a cold frame in early spring

ANEMONES

Anemones (sometimes called Windflowers) hail from temperate regions across Asia and Europe and belong to the buttercup family: look carefully and you will see the resemblance. One of them is bound to suit your garden, whether it has sunny borders or dappled woodland and shady beds.

There are three different types of anemone. The low-growing, spring-flowering species (up to 15cm/6in tall) have daisy-like flowers and bulbous or tuberous roots, and are best planted en masse to carpet dry, sunny spots or in partially shaded, cool woodland areas (depending on the variety). The tuberous Mediterranean 'poppy' varieties (up to 30cm/12in) flower from spring to late summer and are excellent for ground cover in sun or light shade. The third type, the taller, Japanese clump-forming varieties (up to 1.5m/ 5ft), are invaluable for adding height, foliar interest and colour to the late-summer and autumn border.

The flowers vary greatly: they may be saucer-shaped, star-shaped or have double petals. What they have in common is that they are easy to grow, especially the taller border plants, and come in shades of blue, pink, mauve, purple and white.

A. blanda ♀ (5–10cm/2–4in) – *see above* – has vivid blue daisy-like flowers in spring; *A. coronaria* (De Caen Group) 'Die Braut' (30cm/12in) has white flowers from spring to early summer; *A. × hybrida* 'September Charm' (90cm/3ft) has rosy pink flowers, and *A. × h.* 'Honorine Jobert' ♀ (1.5m/5ft) has crisp white flowers, both from late summer to early autumn.

Anemone hupehensis 'Hadspen Abundance' ♀ Japanese anemone

⬆ 60cm–1.2m/2–4ft ⬌ 45cm/18in　　EASY

Japanese anemones are invaluable for the late-summer and autumn border. This Asian offering is an upright, clump-forming herbaceous perennial with suckering shoots and dark green palmate leaves that make pleasing mounds once established. It has tall, branched stems, topped with an abundance of shallow salvers of simple, deep pink five-petalled flowers with soft, fluffy yellow stamens, from mid-summer. *A.h.* var. *japonica* 'Prinz Heinrich' ♀ (90cm/3ft) has semi-double, pale rose pink flowers with yellow centres.

> **BEST USES** Invaluable for foliage and colour in the flower border or a woodland garden; reliable performers in coastal and north-facing gardens

FLOWERS July to September

SCENTED No

ASPECT Any, in a sheltered or exposed position; full sun to partial shade

SOIL Any fertile, humus-rich, well-drained soil

HARDINESS Fully hardy at temperatures down to -15°C/5°F; needs no winter protection

DROUGHT TOLERANCE Medium, once established

PROBLEMS Caterpillars, slugs and snails; leaf spot and powdery mildew

CARE Mulch with organic matter annually in spring; cut back flowering stems in late autumn

PROPAGATION Division in autumn or early spring

Gaura lindheimeri ♀

⬆ 1.5m/5ft ⬌ 90cm/3ft   EASY

This graceful Texan is a clump-forming, bushy perennial with narrow, lance-shaped mid-green leaves on green, slender, arching, trembling stems, with pink-tinged flower buds along the stems. They open to reveal an airy haze of star-shaped white flowers with spidery anthers, from early summer to late autumn and beyond. *G.l.* 'Siskiyou Pink' (50cm/20in) is more compact, with pink flowers; *G.l.* 'Whirling Butterflies' (75cm/30in), with white flowers, is more free-flowering, if that is possible.

> **BEST USES** Gorgeous in the cottage garden or traditional border; mixes well with grasses and naturalised planting; bees and butterflies love it

FLOWERS June to October (up to the first frosts)

SCENTED No

ASPECT South or west facing, in a sheltered position; full sun to partial shade (flowering is reduced in shade)

SOIL Any fertile, well-drained soil

HARDINESS Fully hardy at temperatures down to -15°C/5°F; needs no winter protection

DROUGHT TOLERANCE Excellent, once established

PROBLEMS Aphids; can be short-lived and die off in wet, cold winters

CARE Cut back to just above ground level in early spring when new foliage emerges

PROPAGATION Self-seeds easily once established; division in spring

Kniphofia 'Percy's Pride'
Red-hot poker/Torch lily

⬆ 1.2m/4ft ⬌ 60cm/24in   EASY

Red-hot pokers, originally from Africa, are easily recognisable among the larger herbaceous perennials. They have long, arching, narrow, tough green leaves and tiny, long tubular flowers, densely clustered together to form poker-like flowers, normally in orange and yellow, borne on long, stout, straight stems in summer (often into autumn). This unusual, zingy lime green variety has a plethora of the trademark pokers and is invaluable in the late-summer to autumn border. Look out for the compact *K.* 'Bees' Sunset' ♀ (75cm/30in, orange-gold pokers) and *K.* 'Little Maid' (60cm/24in, pale lemon), both flowering in summer, and the tall *K.* 'Tawny King' (1.2m/4ft), with warm apricot flowers, into autumn.

> **BEST USES** Ideal as focal points in the coastal, gravel or Mediterranean garden; bees love it

FLOWERS July to October

SCENTED No

ASPECT South or west facing, in a sheltered or exposed position; full sun to partial shade

SOIL Any fertile, moist, well-drained soil

HARDINESS Fully hardy at temperatures down to -15°C/5°F; needs no winter protection

DROUGHT TOLERANCE Good, once established

PROBLEMS Thrips

CARE Mulch the base of the plant with organic matter annually in spring; remove faded flower spikes; dry mulch young plants during first winter

PROPAGATION Division in late spring

Solidago 'Golden Wings'
Golden rod/Aaron's rod

⬆ 2m/6ft ⬌ 90cm/3ft   EASY

Originally from North America, this is a tough, upright perennial for problem areas. It is a very fast-growing, bushy, clumping, spreading plant (with invasive tendencies), with fairly ordinary, narrow, lance-shaped mid-green leaves. It's the masses of branching, slightly flattened sprays of small, yellow-gold flowers, borne on tall arching stems in late summer to early autumn, that really commend it. Bee heaven. *S.* 'Goldkind' (syn. *S.* Golden Baby) (30cm/12in), with gold flowers, suits smaller spaces.

BEST USES Ideal for bridging the summer–autumn gap in the flower border; a natural choice for wildlife gardens; plant with tall grasses

FLOWERS September to October
SCENTED No
ASPECT South or west facing, in a sheltered or exposed position; full sun
SOIL Any fertile, well-drained soil; best on sandy soils
HARDINESS Fully hardy at temperatures down to -15°C/5°F, needs no winter protection
DROUGHT TOLERANCE Good, once established
PROBLEMS Powdery mildew
CARE Mulch with organic matter annually in spring, to encourage drought resistance; cut down to just above ground level in spring; may need staking; dig up unwanted clumps as it can be invasive
PROPAGATION Division in autumn or spring

Verbena bonariensis ♟

⬆ 2m/6ft ⬌ 50cm/20in   EASY

This tall, erect, elegant, clump-forming perennial from South America is easy to grow, even from seed, and is a really classy contender. The straight, self-supporting olive grey stems bear very sparse, narrow, lance-shaped leaves, and are topped with branching stems of small, dense heads of lilac-purple flowers that are madly attractive to butterflies and bees.

BEST USES Try these skeletal stems in the middle of the border, rising graciously above lower-growing perennials; ideal for the cottage garden, informal border or Mediterranean garden

FLOWERS June to October
SCENTED No
ASPECT South or west facing, in a sheltered or exposed position, with protection from strong winds; full sun
SOIL Any fertile, well-drained soil; avoid very waterlogged soil
HARDINESS Fully hardy at temperatures down to -15°C/5°F; needs no winter protection
DROUGHT TOLERANCE Excellent, once established
PROBLEMS None
CARE Strong winds can knock this plant sideways, but otherwise self-supporting; cut old stems back to just above ground level in spring, once new basal growth emerges
PROPAGATION Self-seeds easily; sow seed at 21°C/70°F in a greenhouse in spring

WINTER

Winter is tricky for border plants. Most of them like long, warm sunny days, so the herbaceous plant menu is undeniably limited during the winter months. However, that said, there are still a few brave contenders out there just champing at the chance to strut their stuff. They may not be as gaudy or extravagant as earlier season flowerers (winter plants err towards muted restraint), but they are invaluable in keeping the garden tapestry threaded with texture. Like miser's gold, those unexpected splashes of colour bring unforeseen treasure to the winter garden as we head into the chilly, darker days that lie ahead.

Eranthis hyemalis 🎖
Winter aconite

⬆ 5–8cm/2–3in ⬌ 5cm/2in   **EASY**

Winter aconites put in a cheerful appearance in late winter to early spring. This low-growing, clump-forming tuberous perennial from France has simple, cup-shaped buttercup yellow flowers, with a ruff of leaf-like bracts beneath, and lobed, bright green leaves. A lively and reliably uncomplicated plant, it can be placed almost anywhere in the winter garden. *E.h.* 'Flore Pleno' has double yellow flowers with green centres. (All parts of the plant may cause skin irritation.)

BEST USES Ideal for naturalising in a woodland garden or grassy areas; useful colour in borders or under deciduous shrubs and trees; excellent as ground cover on awkward slopes

FLOWERS February to March
SCENTED No
ASPECT Any, in a sheltered or exposed position; full sun to partial shade
SOIL Any fertile, moist, well-drained, humus-rich soil
HARDINESS Fully hardy at temperatures down to -15°C/5°F; needs no winter protection
DROUGHT TOLERANCE Poor
PROBLEMS Slugs and snails; late frosts can damage the leaves and flowers
CARE Best planted into warm soil in autumn to allow tubers to establish; cut back tatty leaves
PROPAGATION Sow ripe seed outdoors in spring; divide tubers after flowering but before leaves die back and replant 5cm/2in deep

Galanthus nivalis ♉
Snowdrop

⬆ 15cm/6in ⬌ 8cm/3in   EASY

This tiny bulbous perennial is found from the Ukraine to the Pyrenees. Much loved, it has short, narrow, fairly upright bladed pale green leaves and smooth, short stalks, each with a fragrant, nodding, pure white cup-shaped flower, with fresh green colouring at the base of each flower bud and matching green banding on the inner petals. *G.n.* 'Viridapice' has pale green markings at the tips of the outer white petals; *G.* 'Atkinsii' ♉ (20cm/8in) is pure white with green banding at the inner tips.

> **BEST USES** Lovely in the cottage garden, or in a shaded north-facing border; does well in containers, placed near the kitchen window or back door, where they can be easily seen and smelled

FLOWERS January to February
SCENTED Yes
ASPECT Any, in a sheltered or exposed position; full sun to partial shade
SOIL Any fertile, humus-rich, well-drained soil
HARDINESS Fully hardy at temperatures down to -15°C/5°F; needs no winter protection
DROUGHT TOLERANCE Poor
PROBLEMS Narcissus bulb fly, slugs and snails
CARE For best results plant after flowering but before leaves die down (when plants are 'in the green'); or plant fresh bulbs about 5cm/2in apart and 5–10cm/2–4in deep, depending on variety, from October to December
PROPAGATION Division after flowering

Helleborus niger ♉
Christmas rose

⬆ 30cm/12in ⬌ 45cm/18in   EASY

Hellebores are marvellous for year-round interest, with interesting flowers, some cupped, others shallow or pendent, ranging in colour from pinks and plums to pale greens and white. This tough evergreen perennial from Europe has serrated, glossy dark green leaves and is a winter treasure. The nodding, bowl-shaped pure white flowers, with long lemony stamens, are produced from early winter to early spring, and the foliage is outstanding for most of the year. 10/10.

> **BEST USES** Perfect for underplanting in shrub borders; terrific for all-year interest in a cottage garden or formal flower border

FLOWERS December to March
SCENTED No
ASPECT Any, in a sheltered position, with protection from strong, cold winds; full sun to partial shade
SOIL Any fertile, moist, humus-rich, well-drained soil
HARDINESS Fully hardy at temperatures down to -15°C/5°F; needs no winter protection
DROUGHT TOLERANCE Good, once established, in partial shade (but not in full sun)
PROBLEMS Aphids, slugs and snails; leaf spot
CARE Remove faded, tatty leaves; mulch the base of the plant with organic matter annually in autumn
PROPAGATION Division after flowering or in autumn; sow ripe seed immediately in pots in a cold frame

Iris unguicularis 🏅
Algerian iris

⬆ 30cm/12in ⬌ 15–30cm/6–12in   **EASY**

This small, rhizomatous perennial iris, from dry rocky areas of Algeria, brings fragrance and colour to the winter landscape with its large, beardless, fragrant purple flowers (about 8cm/3in across) and vivid yellow throats, often appearing in late autumn and continuing into early spring, borne on short stems with strap-like evergreen leaves. It is low maintenance and thrives on next to nothing, accustomed to dearth in its native lands. *I.u.* 'Walter Butt' (30cm/12in) has large lavender flowers from November to February.

> **BEST USES** Ideal for early colour, in a cottage garden or border, or in coastal, gravel or Mediterreanean gardens; deer and rabbit proof; irresistible to bees; excellent as cut flowers

FLOWERS November to March
SCENTED Yes
ASPECT South or west facing, in a sheltered position; full sun
SOIL Any fertile or poor, well-drained soil (good drainage is essential)
HARDINESS Fully hardy at temperatures down to -15°C/5°F; needs no winter protection
DROUGHT TOLERANCE Excellent, once established
PROBLEMS Slugs and snails
CARE Mulch with organic matter annually in spring; flowers are not frost hardy, so cut them in bud and bring indoors
PROPAGATION Division in autumn

Viola odorata 'Wellsiana' 🏅
English violet/Sweet violet

⬆ 8cm/3in ⬌ 15cm/6in   **EASY**

Where would a cottage garden be without violets? There are more than 500 species of these much-loved woodland perennials from temperate regions across the globe. Most flower in spring or summer, but this semi-evergreen rhizomatous variety with a compact, gently spreading habit, and heart-shaped, toothed, bright green leaves, throws out its sweetly scented, dainty purple flowers with careless charm from late winter to spring.

> **BEST USES** Favourites in the cottage garden; do well as ground cover in woodland or to brighten a gloomy area of the garden; good in a wildflower garden, decorating the front of a spring border or in pots in a lightly shaded corner

FLOWERS February to April
SCENTED Sweetly scented flowers
ASPECT Any, in a sheltered or exposed position; full sun to partial shade
SOIL Any fertile, humus-rich, moist, well-drained soil
HARDINESS Fully hardy at temperatures down to -15°C/5°F; needs no winter protection
DROUGHT TOLERANCE Poor
PROBLEMS Slugs and snails; powdery mildew
CARE Trim off spent flowers to limit self-seeding, or leave to encourage spreading
PROPAGATION Self-seeds easily; division in autumn or spring

Planting with perennials

An herbaceous perennial (often known simply as a perennial) is a soft-stemmed, non-woody plant with ornamental flowers that lives for more than one growing season. It produces flowers every year, once established, and usually dies back in autumn, starting to grow again in spring. Some perennials disappear altogether in winter, leaving an empty space, before reappearing in the new season. A few herbaceous perennials are evergreen or semi-evergreen and don't die down in winter (bergenia and hellebore, for example), but these are the exception.

Herbaceous perennials may be bulbous or have rhizomatous, tuberous, tap or fibrous roots, and some have a carpeting nature whilst others are tall and showy, but all behave in the same way: they put out shoots, stems, leaves and flowers in the growing season, and this top-growth dies back when flowering is over (though the evergreen plants keep their leaves) while the roots live on under the ground. Roots are often a clue to drought tolerance. Taprooted plants delve deep in search of water, whereas plants with spreading, fibrous roots absorb water nearer the surface and are more prone to drying out.

Perennials are usually hardy or half hardy. There are some tender perennials too, but these come from warm climates and can't cope with cold, frost and excessively low temperatures.

Designing a flower border

One of the most important ingredients for a successful border is planning.

Whether you are renovating a tired, overgrown border or planting from scratch, a little creative thought will give your flower borders the wow factor.

A colourful mixed border in summer

The tumbling exuberance of a cottage garden

Consider what you want to achieve: year-round interest or a border that is at its best in spring or summer; an overblown sensory garden where flower and scent reign supreme or a low-maintenance contemporary planting scheme. You may be inspired to design your border by colour: white gardens are very popular in spring and early summer, while the blazing reds and fiery oranges of a hot-coloured border come into their own in the late-summer months. Autumn-flowering plants will keep both colour and interest in any border design well into late autumn and often into the early winter months.

It is important to choose plants that suit your garden's aspect and its soil (see pages 105 and 106). When a plant needs well-drained soil, don't even think of sticking it in badly drained sodden ground, for it will surely die. And it is no good putting a sun-lover in the shade and vice versa: it just won't thrive. Take time to have a thoughtful look at your beds or borders and determine where the sun hits them during daylight hours.

Look for plants that offer more than just flower colour: perhaps foliage that colours up in autumn or is evergreen, or interesting seed heads that look good with a touch of frost.

These ingredients help to create depth and give continuity to a planting scheme. Aim for border plants that offer as much as possible in the way of interest, by means of shape, habit, foliage, flower and – naturally – colour.

Form and foliage

Different perennials achieve different effects within the flower border, so by selecting them for specific virtues and blending them together creatively, you can achieve spectacular flower combinations. The arrangement of the plants by both size and habit will give a rhythmic, cohesive plant design. Try out plants that have a spreading or pendulous habit against those with more vertical, upright form.

If you plant a flower border with low-level perennials, all the same colour, with much the same flower and leaf shape, don't be surprised if the border looks dull. But throw in a tall, architectural allium amongst some low-growing brunnera and the arching habit of *Polygonatum odoratum* (Solomon's seal) and immediately you have height, colour and leaf contrast, as well as a succession of flowering.

Good-looking foliage that has a long period of interest will help knit together the overall framework. Aim for a good mix of large-leaved foliage (acanthus, rodgersia and hellebore) with small-leaved plants (alchemilla, lamium and pulmonaria). Some perennials have exceptional foliage but their flowers are insignificant and these have not been widely included in this book. However, that is not to say they aren't useful. They are an invaluable addition for creating texture and providing a backdrop to the more showy flowering perennials in any successful border planting. These include ferns and grasses and very small shrubs, such as traditional ground cover vinca.

One of the most common mistakes when designing flower borders is using single plants in isolation. Plant in groups of odd numbers, say, three, five or seven, for an informal arrangement; planting in even numbers gives the border a more formal appearance. If you long for a riotous cottage garden, you will be planting a jumble of plants at differing heights, with contrasting colours, and their growing habits will differ too. But if you want your border to be more restrained, plant in even numbers, in blocks, and restrict the palette to about three main colours.

Colour

Theming borders by colour is a very natural and effective option, but mixing lots of differently coloured plants together looks frightful, especially when they are dotted about singly: this is why many flower borders never amount to much. Choose a colour theme and stick to it. I know how tempting it is to include just one more colour, but your border will be more successful if you are firm about your colour choices.

However, if the main colours are pink, purple and white, for example, there is nothing to stop you choosing variations of those colours; pale pinks, lilacs, cerise, creams or plummy tones. This will have the effect of harmonising the border. Plant in numbers and try to repeat the more structural plants here and there, or repeat the colours along the length of the bed: it all helps the border to hang together.

White flowers offer a cool, airy lightness and can bring a shard of brightness to a shady border; they shine out in the evening light and go with just about everything, especially silver foliage. Dark blues and mauves are moody and dramatic, but are the first to fade as evening falls. Pastels, such as pale pinks and delicate lilacs, are soothing and allow the eye to travel into the distance, lengthening perspective; whereas bold reds and oranges are at their best in strong sunlight and halt the eye more quickly, shortening the perspective.

Vividly coloured plantings give the impression of warmth and extravagance, whereas cooler colours, such as blues and purples, are more restful. The visual impact in a 'hot' border relies on reds, yellows, oranges and brooding purples, so any muted, pastel or white plants should be avoided. However, dark purples, blacks and deep blues are useful for merging the gap between a hot border and a pastel one. As a general rule of thumb, blues, greens and purples work well together. Throw reds and oranges into this colour combination and you achieve a bolder, more exotic colour scheme.

Making a plan

Grab a pen and paper and make wish lists of plants you really fancy. To gain inspiration, look at gardening books, make seasonal visits to the garden centre (no buying just yet!) or visit gardens that are open to the public. I often see lovely flower combinations in other people's gardens and I jot them down in a notebook for later use.

PLANTS FOR DIFFERENT PURPOSES

Broadstroke plants tend to be structural plants. They often have exceptional, long-lived foliage, but can also be chosen for their strong flower shape and colour. They are the workhorses of garden borders, providing a backdrop of attractive foliage or flower to enhance the other border perennials. They are very effective when repeated throughout the composition, helping to unify it.

Broadstroke plants are undoubtedly one of the most important ingredients in any flower border and have to be hardy and reliable as they are going to be the mainstay of the operation. Achillea, alchemilla, hardy geraniums, hellebores, hostas and rodgersia are just some examples of this type of plant.

Temporary effect plants are short-lived plants that offer a bold splash of colour or have outstanding sculptural quality. Because they are so fleeting in their appearance, they are only really effective when planted against more reliable performers with longer lives.

Foxgloves or Oriental poppies are tall, vertical plants that can add a sense of rhythm and dramatic pace when scattered throughout a flower border but, if planted in isolation, these one-hit wonders fade all too soon: they really need the back-up of broadstroke plants to be shown off at their best.

Don't play safe and leave your taller plants to the back of the border; they can work surprisingly well sited mid-border, and some of the mid-height verbascums and stately summer iris can look fantastic planted nearer the front of a border (though I don't mean right up on the front edge), to give variation to the planting.

Fillers are those modest little perennials, often low-growing, that add a layer of low-level interest to planting schemes. They may lack visual impact when seen in isolation but, grouped together, they are excellent for filling empty gaps whilst waiting for something else to come into bloom, or covering the fading foliage of a plant that has already had its finest hour. They can also offer long-lasting interest, especially if they are semi-evergreen or evergreen. Ajuga, brunnera and lamium are included here.

If you don't feel confident about designing a border from scratch, copy a fetching plant combination from someone else's garden – there is no sincerer form of flattery – but you don't have to mirror these plantings precisely. Take them as a workable rule and then throw in some other plants to make your planting schemes individual. Ask for guidance at the garden centre or local nursery: you'll be surprised how generous people are in sharing their garden prowess.

Look for colours that complement each other, or bold contrasts in colour or leaf shape. Alliums and achilleas are fabulous partners, whilst stately deep blue delphiniums, rising from a bed of airy blue forget-me-nots and *Alchemilla mollis* (Lady's mantle) does the trick for me! And don't forget perfume – so many plants have seductive fragrance.

Now look at your plant list again and edit it: check each plant as a possible contender, making sure it has something special to offer in at least two of the following features:

- foliage
- flower shape
- flower colour
- plant shape and architectural form
- scent

If every plant you choose has two or more strong features, your flower borders will be certain to earn their keep, offering multi-dimensional appeal rather than the fleeting pleasure of an impractical impulse buy.

Great planting schemes don't just happen. Be bold and experimental in your plant choices and don't be afraid to make mistakes: winning planting combinations are achieved through trial and error. Allow your borders to develop, don't make hard and fast rules, experiment with form and flower and you will find that they gradually improve beyond measure.

Aspect

Sun and shade

All plants need direct or indirect sunlight to survive, but the amount of sun they need varies. Some plants love being in full sun, whilst others may be far happier in partial or full shade. It is important to know how much sunlight your garden enjoys when choosing plants, so you can match them up with a planting spot that will suit them: there is more to growing plants than sticking them in the ground in any old place and keeping your fingers crossed.

The direction your garden faces is referred to as its aspect. East-facing beds will be in sun most of the morning, south-facing beds in sun all day and those facing west may get the afternoon and evening sun. North-facing gardens get the least light of all and have a tendency to dampness, so woodland or shade-loving plants often do better in these situations. Whatever its aspect, tall trees or large buildings overlooking the garden can cast it into shade, and garden sheds, garages and outbuildings may create shady patches, so be aware of your garden's cooler spots. Take time to see where the light is throughout the day and at different times of year.

The plant descriptions give plants' preferences for facing north, east, south or west, but many plants are unfussy and will thrive in almost any aspect. Some are more picky. Plants that originally come from the Mediterranean or other warm climes are used to long hours of sunshine and are more likely to succeed in a southerly or west-facing spot. Equally, there are some plants whose leaves bleach or shrivel under the blast of full-strength sunshine; they prefer cooler, shadier conditions. Site your garden plants in their preferred aspect and they will grow happily for you.

Some gardens are vast, with multiple borders enjoying every available aspect, but for most of us the positions of our flower borders come with the house. If you have a choice, site your borders against a west or south-facing wall or fence. The old saying 'west is best' has some foundation, as this is probably the best of all options for growing a wide range of plants.

If you have bought a house with a north-facing aspect, confine yourself to shade-loving plants or plants with large leaves that will thrive in gloomier conditions. Putting plants in pots in an elevated position, such as on a garden table or in a raised border, will help them get their heads nearer the light.

Shelter

Brick walls, fencing, hedges or mature trees and shrubs all create shelter. These boundaries absorb the brunt of the weather, protecting your plants from strong, cold or drying winds. Gardens without shelter take the full force of winds, hard rain, frosts and snow in winter, and drying winds and direct overhead sunlight in the summer months. Frosts are not much of an issue for gardeners in mild areas and city centres, but in colder regions hard frosts in winter and often into spring are par for the course.

Fortunately, most of the border perennials mentioned in this book are fully hardy and need no protection beyond the shelter that most garden environments already provide. For plants that are less hardy, a wall that enjoys long hours of sunshine will have warm soil at its footings and rarely be exposed to any winds at all, providing an ideal mini-environment. Every garden has a sheltered corner somewhere and wise gardeners make good use of these weather sanctuaries wherever possible.

Soil

Most plants need soil to grow: it anchors the plant in the ground and provides it with the nutrients, air and water it needs. A good soil is:

- **moist** – able to retain water, without becoming boggy
- **fertile** – rich in nutrients and able to support new plant growth
- **well drained** – allowing excess surface water to drain away
- **crumbly and open in texture** – allowing roots to grow through it

Different plants prefer different soils and the type and quality of soil is a major factor in growing any plant successfully.

Types of soil

There are four common types of garden soil: sandy, clay, loam and chalk. These differ in their ability to retain water, their nutrient values and in their acidity or alkalinity.

Sandy soil is light, dry, well-aerated soil that is free draining and easy to dig. However, water drains through sandy soil very quickly. Because it doesn't hold moisture and nutrients are easily washed away, it needs to be enriched with organic matter to improve water retention and fertility (unless you are growing plants that like the poor conditions of sandy soil, such as silver-leaved Mediterranean plants and others from similar climates).

Clay soils are wet and heavy to dig in winter but rock hard in times of drought. Because the soil texture is heavy and condensed, the aeration is poor, and many plants struggle to get their roots down into this dense footing. It is slow to warm up in spring, but retains warmth well once the growing season is underway. The plus side of clay soil is that it is high in nutrients and supports a wide selection of plants. Waterlogged clay soils are perfect for plants that like boggy conditions, such as gunneras.

Loam is rich, dark brown in colour, allowing it to absorb the heat of the sun easily, with a crumbly texture. It combines all the good points of clay and sandy soil, without any of the disadvantages. It is easy to dig, has high nutrient levels, good water retention and, because of its friable composition, plant roots become easily established. Most plants thrive in loam.

Asters thrive in fertile, moist, well-drained soil

Chalk (or limestone) soils are very free draining, so they lack fertility, as nutrients get washed away. They can be desert dry in summer and sticky and difficult to work on in winter. Adding organic matter annually is the only reliable method of improving chalky soils, but there are a great many lime-hating plants, so planting choices are limited. Plants that are happy in chalky soils include campanulas and many euphorbias.

Soil acidity or alkalinity can affect your choice of plants. It is measured as the soil's pH, on a scale of 1–14; soil with a pH of 7 is said to be neutral, below 7 is acid and above 7 is alkaline (you can buy a simple kit to test your soil's pH value). Most plants will grow on a pH between 6 and 7, so you don't need to worry about it too much, but some plants are acid-lovers and can't thrive in neutral soils; these are known as ericaceous plants. Avoid them if you have neutral or alkaline soil.

Improving the soil

Although most gardens don't have perfect soil, it is not difficult to improve the soil you have been given. Herbaceous perennials are greedy feeders, and one of the most important things I have learnt is to feed the soil and let the plants take care of themselves. Some gardeners think that foliar liquid feeds will improve their soil. They don't. If your plants look a little yellow or are growing poorly, a quick-fix tonic may help, but it doesn't add any long-term benefit to the soil.

Feeding the soil means improving its structure and texture by adding bulky organic matter, such as well-rotted manure, leafmould or garden compost. This improves the fertility and aeration of the soil, which in turn aids good root growth and seed germination. It also reduces the need for constant watering:

organic matter acts like a sponge, helping the soil to retain water more efficiently.

Digging in horticultural grit or small-sized gravel is invaluable for clay soils that are heavy or compacted. It opens up the soil, allowing water and air to penetrate more freely and improving drainage.

Improving the soil will make it easier to work with and provide a better growing environment for your plants. As a general guide, the following can be done in late winter or early spring:

- **sandy soil** – dig in organic matter
- **clay soil** – dig in grit; dig in organic matter or spread on the surface
- **compacted soil** – dig in grit, and organic matter if needed; rotovate to break up the compacted surface layer
- **wet soil** – dig in grit or gravel; if the soil is very wet, consider digging soakaways, ditches or drains, or plant in raised beds

Organic soil improvers

Farmyard manure must be well rotted (it will have little or no smell) or it can harm your plants. Apply annually as a mulch and soil conditioner, ideally in autumn on clay soil or late winter or early spring for sandy soils, before plants begin growth. If the soil is very heavy, compacted or waterlogged, dig it into the top 30cm/12in of soil in the first year to speed up the process. Otherwise, spread a thick layer (5–8cm/2–3in) over the beds and let nature do the work.

Mushroom compost is light and easy to use. It contains chalk (which is alkaline) and is useful for acid soil, which tends to have poor fertility. Apply as a mulch, spreading a thick layer (5–8cm/2–3in) on the soil (20kg/40lb will cover 1sq m/1sq yd) in autumn on clay soil or late winter or early spring for sandy soils. Leave it on the soil surface as it breaks down very quickly.

A word of caution: do not use mushroom compost to mulch plants that are acid-lovers. If you are gardening on alkaline, neutral or chalky soil, only use mushroom compost every three years or so.

Leafmould (rotted leaves) is rich in humus, beneficial bacteria and industrious micro-organisms. It adds bulk to the soil and improves its texture. To make leafmould, rake fallen leaves together into a heap or put in a wire mesh bin or black bin liners, keeping them separate from other compost as they take longer to rot down. Water them if they are dry and leave for a year or two.

Green waste soil improver is a coarse-textured material that is used to improve soil structure. It is made from recycled domestic green waste that has been composted by local authorities.

Garden compost is plant matter that has been collected together and left to decay. It is an efficient (and free) means of recycling garden waste, and adds bulk and nutrients to the soil. Any plant matter will compost eventually but brown, woody material takes longer to break down than green material.

When making compost, use roughly equal amounts of green and brown plant material, and avoid substances that don't break down (ashes, tins) or attract vermin (food).

Green material includes grass clippings, vegetable peelings, spent bedding plants and soft green, non-woody prunings as well as coffee grounds or teabags. These all rot quickly. Do not add infected plants or perennial weeds such as dandelions or bindweed. Nettles are the exception: being very nitrogenous, they act as compost accelerators.

MAKING COMPOST

There are two ways of making compost. A 'hot' heap is made in one go, using a large quantity of compostable material; it heats up and decays rapidly, and will be ready for use within a few months. 'Cool' heaps are built up in layers as material becomes available and will take a year or so to decay.

Hot heaps Make a thick base layer of woody plants or twigs to aid air circulation and drainage. Fill the bin or build the heap with well-mixed green and brown material, watering as you go. Cover and leave to heat up. Turn the heap after a couple of weeks, mixing well, and add water if it has dried out. Leave for some months until it reaches the desired texture: it should smell earthy, not dank and rotten, and be brown and crumbly. Compost can sometimes be lumpy and twiggy, but is still ready to use.

Cool heaps Start with a base layer as above, add a 40cm/16in layer of mixed composting material above this, and cover. Keep adding balanced ingredients until the bin is full or the heap is too big to be comfortably handled, then leave alone. After about a year, check to see whether the layers are fully rotted. If the top layer has not broken down but the bottom is ready, take out the finished compost and mix the drier, less decayed material back into the heap; add water, replace the lid or cover and wait a few months more.

Brown material includes cardboard, crushed eggshells, shredded paper, straw, wood shavings and tough hedge clippings. Woody material bulks up the finished compost but is slow to decay (chop it up to speed the process). Fallen leaves decay very slowly, and are better used to make leafmould.

Hide compost bins or heaps (which can handle more material) in a corner of the garden, in full sun or partial shade, siting heaps directly on the soil or grass. Compost bins and heaps need lids or a cover; an old piece of carpet works well. For a constant supply of compost, have several heaps or bins: you can use the compost from one while the other is still rotting down.

Growing

They don't come any easier to grow than hardy perennials. Pop them into a suitable spot, water them in well, firm them down and watch them take off!

They may need staking, and cutting back after flowering, with an annual mulch in spring. For the rest of the time they're happy with judicious watering and occasional weeding.

Buying

Generally speaking, perennials are bought in pots. You can buy them in different sizes, but small plants are just fine: they establish better and you have the pleasure of seeing them grow. It may seem difficult to believe that something a few centimetres tall will ever grow to look like the picture on the label, but even young perennials will achieve a good height and spread within a year.

Always buy plants in rude health. If the roots are escaping through the bottom of the pot or the compost is very dry or there are weeds in the compost, walk on by and find something that looks happier. It is far better to choose a smaller plant that has really healthy-looking foliage than something larger with slightly yellowing patches on the leaves.

I won't be thanked for mentioning this, but if in doubt I often up-end the plant into the palm of my hand, to see that the roots are healthy (they can be white or tan, some are fleshy whilst others are more wiry). If the compost is moist all the way through, there are no insect eggs or pests in the soil and the roots look hearty, the chances are the plant is worth buying. A word of warning here: if the grower has only recently transferred a small plant to a larger pot, it won't have rooted in the new container; turn it upside down and you will be faced with a shower of compost all over your shoes and a glaring assistant.

There are so many places to buy good-quality plants. Specialist nurseries offer unusual plants and a wider choice of varieties than is normally available from garden centres, and they are generous about giving cultivation advice. As well as buying from garden centres, you can often find plants at markets and garden open days or beg cuttings from friends.

Planting

Dig a hole large enough to accommodate the plant rootball without forcing it. Offer the pot up to the hole: if it fits loosely into the hole with space to add soil or compost around it, and the soil in the pot is level with the top of the hole, the hole is big enough for the new plant.

I always add a handful of garden compost or well-rotted manure to the planting hole, regardless of whether I have recently improved the soil. Plants seem to like it (unless they are silver-leaved, which prefer a poor soil) and I believe it helps them settle down more quickly.

Most plants appreciate a good drink before planting. Give them a thorough soaking while they are still in the pot or dunk them in a bucket of water for half an hour, so the water really saturates the roots.

When planting container-grown plants, turn the plant upside down, cupping the foliage with your hand for support, and gently ease the plant from the pot, taking care not to disturb the rootball too much. Plants grown in pots often have roots that look tightly bound and are wrapped in circles: gently tease them apart and spread them in the planting hole.

If the weather is dry, puddle the plant in by pouring a healthy draught of several litres

BULBOUS PERENNIALS

Bulbs are available seasonally, ready for their planting times: plant spring-flowering bulbs from September (tulips are better planted in December), summer-flowering bulbs in early spring and autumn-flowering bulbs in late summer.

It is important to buy cultivated bulbs from reputable sources, as many bulbous plants are threatened in the wild. Check that bulbs are firm and undamaged, not shrivelled or soft to the touch, and try to plant them out within two weeks of buying, before they start shooting.

When planting bulbs in a border, aim for a natural effect rather than planting in straight lines: drop a handful and plant them where they fall. For a more formal effect, plant in loose clumps to maximise their colour impact..

As a rule of thumb, plant bulbs at two or three times their own depth, and a similar distance apart, with the pointed end upward. Some bulbs don't have an obviously pointed end, so if in doubt plant on their sides and leave them to find their own way up. Cover with soil and firm well. Mark where they are with plastic plant labels, to avoid digging them up by mistake.

Deadhead flowers regularly, but leave foliage to die down naturally before removing. Leave in the border for next year, or lift and store in a dry place.

To propagate overcrowded clumps, dig up when the plants are dormant (after the foliage has died down) and separate out the small, undeveloped offsets or bulblets. Replant any good-sized bulbs straight away, but pot up the smaller bulblets and leave in a greenhouse to grow on for 1–2 years before planting out.

of water into the planting hole and letting it drain away before backfilling the hole with soil. Firm the plant down really well with your hands after planting and water again: this ensures the roots make good contact with the soil, and will encourage the plant to 'take root' more effectively.

Staking

Many herbaceous perennials need staking for support. Some flop over in wet weather or become top heavy when in flower; others grow tall or cannot withstand strong winds.

Staking is best done when planting (you might forget later) or in early spring, when new growth will soon mask the supports. It is more difficult to do if you leave it later, and the plants will look choked and bound.

All sorts of staking materials are available from bamboo canes to twiggy pea sticks or ready-made plant supports for specific plants, like peonies. Single canes are suitable for single-stemmed plants such as delphiniums (push the cane deep into the ground and tie the plant loosely to it with twine), or can be placed in a circle round multi-stemmed plants.

Delphiniums may need staking: if so, use single canes

Mulching

To mulch perennials, spread a 5–8cm/2–3in layer of organic matter (such as well-rotted manure, leafmould, mushroom compost or garden compost) on the surface of the beds in early spring or late autumn every year. Plants that like woodland conditions or need reliably moist soil will particularly appreciate being mulched with leafmould.

Make sure the soil is moist and spread the mulch all over the whole surface of the beds rather than just round the base of individual plants: mulching feeds the soil as well as the plant.

Watering

We all need to preserve water in the soil as efficiently as possible and use available water supplies resourcefully. Adding organic matter to the soil by digging it in and by mulching helps enormously in improving the soil's ability to retain moisture, and is the first line of defence in conserving water.

Place water butts around the garden or strategically near guttering and downpipes from the house or greenhouse to catch rainwater (but avoid using rainwater on young seedlings, as it can cause fungal disease).

Water in the early hours of the morning or in late evening, when there is less risk of wastage from evaporation, about three times a week: generous, regular watering encourages plants to root deeply; watering lightly or too frequently can lead to plants making shallow roots near the surface. Shallow-rooted plants are the first to thirst and keel over in dry periods. Water more often in very dry weather or in drought. Wilting plants are a sure sign that the bed needs watering, but if you're not sure whether your plants are short of water, poke a finger right into the soil: if it feels moist you probably don't need to water.

Water at a leisurely pace, so you know you are being thorough. Large gardens can take hours to water properly, so think about installing an inexpensive watering system, such as a leaking hose. This gently seeps water along the length of the beds, and can be placed on top of the soil or shallowly under it, and looped around new plants. Water is delivered directly to the plants, and it can be used in conjunction with a timer.

DRY MULCHES

Use horticultural fleece, dried leaves, old fern fronds or straw as a dry mulch for vulnerable plants when temperatures fall. Tuck the mulch around the base of the plants or place about 10cm/4in of material on top of the plant (the crown) and firm it down gently. This will give protection from snowfall, frost and wet.

ORGANIC AND INORGANIC MULCHES

Mulching with **organic soil improvers**
- increases the soil's fertility
- improves the soil's ability to retain water
- traps moisture at plants' roots, where it can be taken up more effectively
- reduces water evaporation from the soil surface
- suppresses weeds by blocking out light to weed seed
- helps the soil absorb the sun's warmth, which leads to good root establishment

Some organic mulches do not improve the soil: cocoa shells and ornamental bark rob nitrogen from the soil while they are breaking down. They can be decorative and will suppress weeds but are not soil conditioners.

Inorganic mulches such as gravel or granite chippings reduce water loss and keep weeds down, but they do not feed the soil and are essentially decorative.

Weeding

Weeds are wild flowers growing where you don't want them, but they rob garden plants of light, water and nutrients, so like it or not, weeding is a necessary chore. Prevent them establishing by removing annual weeds before they have time to flower and set seed. Dig up perennial weeds such as nettles, removing roots carefully; small pieces of root left in the soil can grow into new plants.

Weedkillers can't tell the difference between treasured garden plants and weeds, and may leave residues in the soil. Healthy soil leads to healthy plant growth; if you can do without weedkillers, your garden will be a better place.

Deadheading

Deadheading is easy: just cut, snap or pinch off faded or dead flowers. Almost all herbaceous perennials benefit from this

Agapanthus grow well in containers

CONTAINER PLANTING

Planting perennials in containers is a great way of extending colour throughout the year: use planted pots to fill bare spaces in the border. Pots are also ideal for making a garden in paved areas, where real borders are simply not possible. When planting in containers:

- choose frostproof pots
- lay crocks at the bottom over the drainage holes
- use a good multi-purpose compost or home-made garden compost, but don't use old compost
- mix water-swelling granules with the compost (about 1g per litre of compost): these reduce the need for constant watering
- cover the soil surface with a layer of leafmould, mushroom compost, decorative gravel or bark to reduce water evaporation

Plants in pots dry out much more quickly than those planted in the ground. Water generously when necessary (this could be every other day but, if you have used water granules, once a week should be sufficient) and ensure the water is soaking through to the roots. The compost should feel damp to the touch, but not waterlogged. Sometimes the compost gets a dry cap or crust, preventing water reaching the roots: a drop of washing-up liquid in the watering can will break the surface tension.

Plants in containers soon use up the nutrients in their soil, so top-dress the surface of the compost each year with a few handfuls of fresh compost, use slow-release fertiliser pellets or apply an annual liquid feed.

Container plants are particularly susceptible to vine weevil, so check pots regularly. A drench to treat and prevent infestations is available from garden centres.

Pull up any weeds as you spot them.

procedure, which serves two purposes: plants look tidier and, more importantly, some will produce a second flush of flowers once deadheaded.

Once they have flowered, plants produce seed. However, deadheading removes these potential new seeds, effectively telling the plant to go back and start again, and tricking it into concentrating its energy on new growth (and more flowers for some) instead of directing it into seed production.

Leave some flowers if you want to collect seed from a particular plant, and don't deadhead plants if you want them to self-seed around the garden. Where plants have attractive seed heads, leave these alone as well.

Cutting back

Most perennials die down after the growing season has finished, with the onset of autumn or winter weather. Remove dead or decaying material in autumn or spring to keep plants looking tidy and prevent pests or diseases taking up residence in the dying foliage.

Cutting plants back also encourages them to make strong roots and new growth. Cut them just above soil level, leaving the tops of the stems poking out from the ground: grasp several stems at once and cut cleanly, using a sharp pair of secateurs with clean blades, repeating the process through a large clump. Some perennials (such as eryngiums and sedums) start making new basal shoots this year for next year, once flowering is over; trim these back, being careful not to cut into the new growth.

Hardy geraniums benefit from being cut back after the first flowers have faded, and will often produce new shoots and a second, more modest, flush of flowers later in the season.

Leave plants that have particularly attractive skeletal winter shape. Unless they are spring-flowerers, you can cut plants back just as effectively in spring, cutting above any new shoots.

Deadheading hardy geraniums

Hardiness

Happily, the majority of border perennials are tough as old boots and don't need extra protection in winter, so we need only concern ourselves with the following ratings (which follow the RHS hardiness zones).

Fully hardy: hardy to -15°C/5°F
This term describes perennials that are tough enough to withstand a lowest winter temperature of -15°C/5°F without lasting detriment. Plants in this category originate from cold climates and are adept at coping with cold, winds and frosts.

Frost hardy: hardy to -5°C/23°F
Plants in this category can withstand temperatures as low as -5°C/23°F, but once the temperature dips below this, especially for any length of time, the plant may suffer lasting harm or death. Protect with horticultural fleece (available from all garden centres) or provide shelter, such as a greenhouse or cold frame, to prevent roots being frozen or top-growth being seriously damaged by frosts.

Borderline
Despite being rated as fully or frost hardy, some plants may still need protection in winter, especially in cold or exposed areas. Put them in a sheltered spot, cover with a dry mulch or wrap with horticultural fleece, straw or bubble wrap.

Half hardy: hardy to 0°C/32°F
Plants in this category can withstand temperatures down to 0°C/32°F, but not below. Protect with fleece or provide frost-free shelter, such as a porch, frost-free greenhouse or conservatory, where the temperature never falls below freezing.

Problems

Every garden falls prey to pests or diseases at one time or another, but hardy perennials suffer from these problems far less than other plants, which is great news for gardeners. And many ailments can be prevented by employing old-fashioned plant husbandry. There is no substitute for vigilance. Keep a watchful eye on your plants and you will spot problems before they get out of control.

Leaf and stem pests

Pests usually leave obvious signs of their presence, such as chewed leaves, or they can even be caught mid-nibble. Here are some of the most common garden pests you may encounter, with suggestions for dealing with them.

Aphids are a group of pests such as blackfly, greenfly and whitefly, about 3mm/⅛in long, with transparent green, black or white bodies, which occur in large numbers, never in isolation, and are sapsuckers. Feeding on the sap of young shoots causes the leaves and stems of a plant to curl and distort, and damages new emerging growth.
Solution Spray as needed with a few drops of washing-up liquid mixed with water. Alternatively, use a proprietary insecticide.

Capsid bug is a pale green sap-sucking bug, some 6mm/¼in long, which damages leaf tips and peppers leaves with tiny holes. Flowers may also be damaged or distorted.
Solution Use a proprietary insecticide.

Caterpillars are usually easily visible to the naked eye (silky webbing on leaves is also an indicator of their presence) and eat unsightly holes in plant leaves.

Solution Remove by hand. For a large infestation on relatively few leaves, remove the leaves and destroy them. Chemical controls are available.

Earwigs are familiar brown insects, just under 2cm/¾in long, with a set of pincers at the rear. They tend to feed at night, nibbling leaves and flowers, so it is difficult to prevent them unless you are prepared to stake out the garden at midnight.
Solution The damage is marginally unsightly, but is hardly worth getting concerned about. The large amount of leaf growth generated throughout the growing season will invariably disguise the odd chewed leaf.

Eelworms are microscopic nematodes inhabiting the stems and leaves of annual and perennial phlox and other alpines and perennials. Symptoms include stunted, distorted stems and shoots that die back, failing to flower.
Solution Dig up and burn or otherwise dispose of affected plants. There are no chemical or biological controls available.

Leaf miners are the larvae of beetles, moths and flies. They mine through plant leaves, leaving telltale brown and white tunnel patterns on the surface.
Solution Pick off the affected leaves and dispose of them (if you have a bonfire, burn them). Alternatively, use a proprietary insecticide.

Leafhoppers are green, sap-sucking insects, about 3mm/⅛in long, that hop from foliage when the leaves are disturbed. They cause mottling and yellowy discoloration of the leaves, but the damage is not serious.
Solution Use sticky flypaper or spray with a proprietary insecticide.

Narcissus bulb fly can affect daffodils, snowdrops and irises. It is a small, hovering, bumble bee-like fly that lays its eggs at the crown of the bulb. The resulting maggots bore into the bulb, feeding on the flesh. Affected bulbs produce very few leaves and no flowers.
Solution Dig up affected bulbs and dispose of them; plant new bulbs elsewhere. Always buy fresh, firm, disease-free bulbs and avoid planting bulbs that have a spongy or hollow feel. Place soil over the withered foliage to deter the fly from laying eggs.

Narcissus eelworms are microscopic eelworms or nematodes, invisible to the naked eye, which inhabit bulbs of daffodils, bluebells and snowdrops. Initial symptoms are distorted and yellowed growth above ground; bulbs will eventually rot. If you suspect your plants are affected, cut through a bulb and look for concentric brown ringing. Eelworms can spread through the soil to neighbouring plants.
Solution Dig up and burn or otherwise dispose of affected plants. Do not replant the area with bulbs susceptible to eelworms for two years. Always buy healthy bulbs from a reputable source. There are no chemical or biological controls available.

Sawfly larvae are small, green or grey caterpillars which graze on the leaves of many different plants, eventually reducing them to a skeleton of veins. The caterpillars can be found at the leaf edges.
Solution Pick off caterpillars by hand (they wave their back ends in the air when cornered!). Alternatively, spray with a pyrethrum product.

Scarlet lily beetle is a bright red beetle, about 6mm/¼in long, that lays its eggs on the undersides of lily leaves. Adult beetles

and grubs both eat holes in the leaves, so that the following year's bulbs may be undersized and fail to flower.
Solution Spray leaves with olive oil or neem oil to prevent infestations. Pick off bugs by hand and remove any leaves with eggs underneath. Alternatively, use a proprietary insecticide.

Slugs and snails have a legendary appetite for leaf and flower material and remedies for dealing with them vary greatly in their effectiveness. Look for slime trails and leaf damage: leaf damage close to the bottom of the plant is more likely to be caused by slugs, and top leaf damage by snails.
Solution Fill a small plastic tray with beer or sugar water and place it shallowly in the soil at the base of a plant. The slugs and snails are lured by the sugary liquid and drown before they begin their ascent up the plant. Alternatively, sprinkle slug pellets sparingly around the base of plants. Biological controls are also available.

Thrips are more commonly known as thunderflies. They are black insects up to 2mm/¹⁄₁₆in long and feed on the leaf surface, leaving silvery patches and black dottings. They can also feed on flower petals, leaving much the same markings.
Solution Use an organic insecticide or nematode. Alternatively, use a proprietary insecticide.

Vine weevil most commonly affect plants grown in containers and pots, but can also damage plants growing in open ground. The adult beetle is easily recognised by its long pointed snout, and feeds voraciously on the foliage of herbaceous plants and shrubs, making notches along the leaf edges. This is unattractive, but rarely fatal. The real damage is done by their larvae, which feed on the roots of plants. The first noticeable signs of the larvae may be yellowing leaves, poor growth and a wilting plant that does not respond to watering. More often there is very little warning and it is not uncommon to see an otherwise healthy plant suddenly keel over.
Solution A nematode is available; this is a form of parasitic microscopic eelworm that enters the larvae and releases bacteria that kill the grubs. To add to their effectiveness, the nematodes keep reproducing inside the dead grub. Alternatively, water pots with a chemical drench.

Plant diseases

Plant diseases can be harder for the budding gardener to spot than some of the common garden pests but, happily, perennials suffer from fewer diseases than most other plants.

Botrytis **(grey mould)** is a very common fungal disease that strikes plants that are in poor health and flourishes in damp conditions or where air circulation is poor. Grey, fluffy mould containing spores is clearly evident on the plant and, if handled carelessly, will disperse in the air. It can also enter plants through wounds, which may cause leaves to brown and soften before becoming covered in the grey mould. It can survive on live plants and dead or decaying plant tissue and affects many plants, including bulbs and perennials.
Solution It is difficult to control as it is spread through the air, but good growing conditions and plant hygiene do much to prevent its occurrence. Remove all affected parts of the plant, cutting right back to healthy growth. Burn infected material or dispose of in a bin, but do not add to the compost heap.

TIPS FOR DISEASE-FREE PLANTS

- Choose the right plant for the site: a shade-loving plant will struggle in a warm sunny position and be more vulnerable to infection.
- Buy healthy plants and grow disease-resistant varieties wherever possible.
- Wash pots and seed trays before potting up new plants or seedlings.
- Avoid planting too closely together: this improves air circulation round plants.
- Feed and water plants regularly: this equips them with stronger resistance to disease.
- Mulch plant roots to prevent them drying out.
- Clear up dead or damaged leaves where fungal diseases can overwinter.

Clubroot is a soil-borne infection that is almost impossible to control as spores remain in the ground for years and are carried on boots and tools. Symptoms include wilting leaves and yellowing, stunted growth. Affected plants have swollen, club-like roots.
Solution Remove and burn all affected plants. When growing plants from seed, use fresh, sterilised compost and well-scrubbed pots. A clubroot drench or dip is available.

Crown rot and **stem rot** are fungal diseases, spread by water, that attack plants at their roots or above the soil. Roots grow poorly, blacken and become brittle and leaves are stunted or discoloured. Rots can spread rapidly through the plant until it collapses and dies.
Solution Dig up and dispose of rotten plants. Improve drainage and plant at the same depth as the pot, not too deeply.

Downy mildew is a fungal disease affecting annuals and perennials and is less common than powdery mildew. Leaves develop brown and yellow blotches, and their undersides have a fuzzy white growth. If left untreated, the whole plant may die.
Solution Remove any affected leaves immediately, water at the base of plants rather than overhead, thin leaves to improve air circulation and avoid planting too closely together.

Leaf spot is caused by bacteria or fungi and affects many plants. Brown patches appear on the leaves and gradually spread.
Solution Remove affected leaves immediately and burn or dispose of in a bin. Thin leaves to improve air circulation and avoid planting too closely together.

Narcissus basal rot is a serious, soil-borne fungal disease that affects narcissi. The bulbs are infected through their roots or small wounds. Foliage can yellow early and plants may not flower. Bulbs become slightly soft and brown as the rot spreads.
Solution Lift infected bulbs and discard. Lift healthy bulbs immediately after flowering and store them with a dusting of sulphur at temperatures below 22°C/72°F, or replant in another spot, free of the disease. Buy disease-resistant bulbs and discard any damaged bulbs.

Onion white rot is a soil-borne fungal disease, prevalent in wet, cool summers, that affects members of the onion family, including alliums. A fluffy white mould covers the base of the bulb; the leaves yellow and plants may wilt.
Solution Dig up affected bulbs immediately and burn or dispose of in a bin, but don't add to the compost heap. Avoid planting similar bulbs in the same place for eight years. No controls are available to the domestic gardener.

Peony wilt is a fungal disease affecting the base of peony stems, covering them in grey mould. It can strike just before the flower buds open. If left untreated, the plant collapses and dies.
Solution If a whole plant is stricken, dig it up and burn or dispose of in a bin, but don't add to the compost heap. If only some stems are affected, cut them out below soil level and dispose of them. Thin leaves to increase air circulation and don't overwater or overfeed with nitrogenous feeds. No controls are available to the domestic gardener.

Powdery mildew is a common fungal disease that affects many plants and arises from poor growing conditions and poor air circulation. It is easily recognisable as a white powdery substance on the leaves, which will turn leaves brown if left untreated, and results in stunted or distorted growth.
Solution Remove all affected parts of the plant. Water plants regularly. Improve air circulation by thinning leaves; avoid planting too closely together. Proprietary fungicidal sprays are available, but prevention is always better than cure.

Rust is a fungal disease found in moist, damp conditions. Round patches of orangey brown pustules develop on the undersides of leaves. If rust is left unchecked, the life of the plant is at risk.
Solution Hygiene is the surest way to limit rust. Remove infected leaves from the plant and pick up all fallen leaves before they decompose and spread the infection; burn infected material if possible.

Stem rot *see* **Crown rot**

The tell-tale signs of powdery mildew on aquilegia leaves

Tulip fire is a fungal disease that affects tulips, resulting in misshapen leaves with rotting brown patches. Left to fester, both flowers and foliage may wilt and rot. Flower buds may fail to open or have white blotches on the petals.
Solution Dig up and dispose of affected plants, together with the soil around the roots. Don't replant in the same place for two years. Buy healthy, disease-free bulbs.

Verticillium **wilt** is caused by a fungus. The plant's roots die and it collapses for no apparent reason. If a plant wilts for no obvious reason, cut through the stems, which may reveal telltale brown striping.
Solution Dig up affected plants and burn them. Don't plant similar plants in the same place for several years. There are no chemical controls available to the domestic gardener.

Propagation

There are many ways to go about raising new plants but the process is relatively simple for hardy perennials: you can divide larger plants, grow new plants from seed or take cuttings.

Dividing perennials

Division is one of the easiest, most foolproof ways to multiply plants, requiring very little skill to get good results first time. It is normally carried out after flowering in spring but can also be done in autumn, when the soil is still warm, encouraging plants to develop new roots before the onset of winter.

Choose a large clump and dig it up, roots and all. Prise the rootball apart into two halves, using two garden forks back to back. If it is a very large clump, repeat this process to make a number of smaller clumps, all with good visible root systems, or use a sharp knife to cut through tough, fibrous roots. To divide a smaller clump, use a knife or tease the roots apart by hand.

It is best to replant sections taken from the outer edges of a clump and discard the older, tougher centres. Plant out the divided segments in their final positions straightaway if they are large enough, or grow them on in individual pots of compost until they are ready to transplant.

To divide a plant that has tuberous or rhizomatous roots, dig it up and shake the soil from the roots so you can see what you are doing. Cut the roots into pieces, making sure each new piece contains at least one growth bud, and replant.

Sometimes the plant profiles in this book tell you a plant 'resents disturbance' and then suggest you propagate it by division, which seems a contradiction in terms. Where a plant is a little surly about being divided, carry out the operation as gently as possible.

When replanting the divided clumps, firm them in well, give them a good watering and add a mulch of organic matter to help them get over the shock. Don't expect them to be at their best the following growing season: they will take a while to settle down and grow happily again.

Echinops, euphorbias, gauras and hardy geraniums are examples of the many plants that can be multiplied by division.

Growing perennials from seed

Growing plants from seed usually starts in autumn or spring. Seeds of many hardy perennials can be sown in pots and placed in a cold frame or sown in trays or pots in an unheated greenhouse, porch or draught-free windowsill. Seeds of some plants, such as foxgloves and aquilegias, are sown in situ, straight into their final flowering positions in the ground, and many plants self-seed so freely that there is no need to sow them at all.

Collecting and saving seed

You don't always have to buy seed. Seed collected from plants in the garden is free, and it's a fun way of raising multiple new plants from old favourites for next to nothing. Always collect seed from healthy plants. Remember that seed taken from hybrid plants won't necessarily come true: the shape, colour and flowers of the new plant may vary from those of the plant the seed came from.

Collect seed in summer and autumn, when the flowers have come and gone and the seed heads are brown, dry and brittle. These are the ones to collect, as the seed inside will be ripe, and ready for sowing. If the seed heads are still green, bring them inside to dry out before storing them, as they will surely rot with the onset of winter if left outside.

Inula hookeri is prolifically self-seeding

Crack open the dry seed cases or rub them between your fingers to release the seed inside over a piece of newspaper. Separate the chaff from the seed, and either sow immediately or store the seed in small, brown paper envelopes (not plastic bags, as this will make them rot). Label and date each envelope. Store the sealed envelopes in an airtight container until ready for sowing, usually in spring.

Sowing seed

Seeds for most of the plants in this book can be sown in pots (sowing three or four seeds to each pot) and placed in a cold frame for protection. Alternatively, sow in seed trays, placed on a windowsill or in a frost-free lean-to or porch, or into pots in a heated

COLD FRAMES

Cold frames look like mini greenhouses and are used to give a good start to seed that can be sown outdoors: sow seed into pots and place inside the cold frame. They are also useful for hardening off seedlings sown in a greenhouse: transfer the seedlings to the cold frame and leave it open in daylight hours but closed at night. If a cold snap is forecast, tuck some fleece round the edges of the cold frame for extra insulation.

propagator. Sowing times for individual plants are given in their profiles, or will be found on the seed packet if you are using bought seed.

Fill the pots or seed trays with fresh, unused compost to about 6mm/¼in below the rim and press the compost down firmly. Water the compost lightly before sowing the seed thinly, and cover with a fine dusting of compost (using a soil sieve can ensure even coverage). Water regularly with a watering can with a 'rose' fitting, so it doesn't wash the seeds into puddles, and keep the soil moist but not waterlogged; whatever you do, don't let it dry out. Label the pots or trays with the date sown and the name of the plant, to avoid getting mixed up.

Place seed trays or pots in a light, non-draughty spot and wait for the seeds to germinate. If you are sowing in a greenhouse, a light drench of Cheshunt compound watered over the compost before sowing can help prevent 'damping off' (a fungal condition that kills off young seedlings grown under cover).

Caring for seedlings

Once your seedlings appear, water them regularly. Avoid drowning them by using a 'rose' on the watering can. Seedlings are very fragile at this stage, and need careful handling. If the seeds were sown in a heated propagator, open the vents on the propagator once they have sprouted.

As the seedlings grow bigger, they will become overcrowded, with each seedling competing for nutrients and space. It is time to pot them up separately, allowing them the luxury of their own dedicated pot so they have room to develop. This is known as 'pricking out'. Select the healthiest seedlings and pot them up individually in fresh compost, firming each seedling gently into its pot. Water regularly. Always handle seedlings carefully, picking them up by the leaves,

The following are the easiest and most reliable types of cutting for perennials.

Basal stem cuttings are taken from young shoots at the base of the plant, in mid-spring. Detach a short stem with new leaves attached, 5–8cm/2–3in long. With a sharp knife, trim the bottom of the cutting below a node, dip into hormone rooting powder (optional) and pot up in prepared compost; water and label clearly.

Stem-tip cuttings are taken from soft young growth at the tip of a non-flowering shoot, at any time during the growing season. Make a straight cut below a leaf joint (node), remove the leaves from above the leaf joint, leaving two or three leaves at the top. The final cutting should be about 5cm/2in long and have two or three pairs of leaves.

Root cuttings are taken from vigorous young roots when the plant is dormant, usually in winter. They are used for plants that produce suckers or shoots from the root area, such as acanthus or Oriental poppies.

Choose a root about 10cm/4in long and as thick as a pencil. Cut the root into sections, each about 4cm/1½in long, using straight cuts at the top end and diagonal at the bottom. Wash off the soil, pat dry with a paper towel and dust the cuttings with a fungicide (available from garden centres). Insert each cutting into a prepared pot of compost diagonal end first, leaving the flat end just visible above the surface. Cover with a thin layer of sharp sand, water and label.

never the stem, as this may damage them.

If you have sown into pots in a cold frame, wait until your seedlings have four good seed leaves and either pot them into separate containers to grow them on into larger plants, or harden them off over a three-week period before planting them out. Be aware that young plants are more prone to slug and snail attacks than mature plants: I grow my plants to a reasonable size before planting them into their final spaces in late spring or early summer.

Growing perennials from cuttings

Most perennials are easy to propagate from cuttings, which is very handy if your herbaceous perennials aren't yet large enough to divide. A cutting is a small piece of stem or root, cut from an existing plant and grown on in a separate pot to produce a new plant, exactly like the one it was taken from.

Always choose your cutting material from a healthy, vigorous plant and try to take cuttings in the morning, when plants are more turgid and full of water.

Caring for cuttings
Once you have taken your cuttings, place them in a light, frost-free spot. Keep them watered and leave them to increase in size. If you have grown your cuttings indoors, they will need a period of hardening off.

The gardening year

Spring

Spring is the beginning of the flowering year for many perennials. Mulch all the beds with organic matter early on and keep abreast of weeds, which begin their relentless march even this early in the year.

Remember the three Ds: remove any dead, diseased or damaged material. Cut back scruffy, frost-damaged leaves to just above ground level to encourage new healthy growth as the weather warms and the days lengthen.

Spring is a good time to establish new plants, transplant home-grown plants from the cold frame or start seed sowing. You can take many cuttings now too. Look carefully at your plant groupings. If a particular combination didn't quite work last year, be brave: grab a spade, dig plants up and move them about to create a more complementary grouping. Spring division is very successful, so take a look at which perennials you might like to increase and divide them now.

Early to mid-spring is an ideal time to plant summer-flowering bulbs. Leave spring-flowering bulbs to die back naturally, masked by the burgeoning foliage and spread of later plants.

Stake any plants that will need support as they grow taller: early staking always looks more natural, allowing plants to grow up against their stakes, covering unsightly twine or bamboo canes.

Have a spring clean: clear out the greenhouse and potting shed, wash out the pots you are going to use for seed sowing, and check that all the watering systems are working. Get the lawnmower serviced and sharpen your secateurs.

Summer

Many people don't bother doing too much in the summer garden, as annual summer holidays take precedence, but newly planted perennials can be particularly vulnerable to water shortages, so keep a watchful eye and water them regularly to help them establish.

By now many of the spring-flowering perennials have done their thing. Cut back early-flowering plants once their flowers have faded for a second flush later on. Don't be afraid to add annuals and bedding plants into gaps in the border, to keep the whole display going.

Note which plant combinations looked good and earmark those that haven't quite worked, with a view to changing them around in autumn for a more compatible composition. Be critical about this and don't be afraid to move things: none of us likes upheaval but quite often we find, with hindsight, that a move was the best thing for us. Plants benefit from the same treatment.

Late summer is an ideal time to plant autumn-flowering bulbs, such as cyclamen.

Autumn

If your garden is already over, make a note to buy yourself some choice autumn-flowering plants to extend your garden's interest next season.

Autumn can see us basking in the mellow heat of an Indian summer or wintry fingers may be clutching at the stems of plants, so be prepared: an unexpected dash around with emergency fleece for plants that need a bit of extra protection may prove just as necessary as keeping plants supplied with water in the heat.

This is another good time to plant, but don't leave it too late in the year: planting while the soil is still warm will help plants establish more quickly. Move the plants that you earmarked in the summer, and divide large perennials that have outgrown their allotted space, such as border phlox, saxifrage and lychnis. Take root cuttings of acanthus or Oriental poppies.

Now that most plants have flowered and are dying back, you can cut everything back and put the garden to bed for the winter. But don't forget to start planting spring-flowering bulbs, as these will help to create layers of interest to the border design.

Winter

October to December is the ideal time for planting many tulips and daffodils for flowering in spring. But as the winter weather sets in, check your cold frames if you are overwintering cuttings from earlier in the year and provide extra insulation if need be, with bubble wrap, fleece or sacking lining the cold frame to give extra warmth.

Birds will be hopping about scavenging for winter berries, so install a well-placed bird feeding table so you can enjoy their cheeky activity. Come spring they will obligingly help out by gobbling up a fair amount of plant predators. Money in the bank!

Winter is a great time for reflecting on the past gardening year. How did your garden fare? If you had more or less continual interest in the garden from spring to autumn, you have designed your borders well. If there were weeks where there was very little to look at and dull, empty patches yawned open, there is still room for improvement. The most wondrous thing about each new gardening year is that it allows us the luxury of doing things differently. We get a unique second chance to right the blunders of yesterday.

A tangle of verbena in autumn

Border perennials for specific purposes

The following lists are designed to help you choose the right border plants for your garden space. Let your creative juices loose and experiment with colour combinations, texture, fragrance and shape. A little planning goes a long way and will reward you with stunning borders through the year.

Fragrance
Achillea 'Summerwine'
Agastache 'Blue Fortune'
Allium 'Globemaster'
A. schubertii
A. sphaerocephalon
Anemone sylvestris
Chaerophyllum hirsutum
   'Roseum'
Convallaria majalis
Crambe cordifolia
Crinum × powellii
Cyclamen hederifolium
Cynara cardunculus
Dianthus 'Becky Robinson'
Dictamnus albus var.
   purpureus
Echinacea purpurea 'Robert
   Bloom'
Filipendula purpurea
Galanthus nivalis
Hemerocallis 'Whichford'
Hesperis matronalis
Iris 'Dusky Challenger'
I. 'Sultan's Palace'
I. unguicularis
Lilium 'Miss Lucy'
Lunaria rediviva
Lupinus 'The Governor'
Maianthemum racemosum
Monarda 'Cambridge Scarlet'
Nepeta × faassenii
Nerine bowdenii
Oenothera fruticosa
   'Fyrverkeri'
Paeonia 'Claire de Lune'
P. lactiflora 'Duchesse de
   Nemours'
Phlomis russeliana
Phlox paniculata 'Bright Eyes'
Phuopsis stylosa 'Purpurea'
Polygonatum odoratum
Primula vulgaris
Salvia × sylvestris 'Mainacht'
Sanguisorba 'Tanna'
Tellima grandiflora
Tulbaghia violacea 'Alba'

Viola odorata 'Wellsiana'

Full shade
Bergenia 'Bressingham
   White'
Convallaria majalis
Dracunculus vulgaris
Gentiana asclepiadea
Heuchera 'Persian Carpet'
Kirengeshoma palmata
Lamium maculatum 'Beacon
   Silver'
Liriope muscari
Maianthemum racemosum
Podophyllum peltatum
Polygonatum odoratum
Primula vulgaris
Pulmonaria 'Sissinghurst
   White'
Tiarella wherryi
Tricyrtis formosana 'Dark
   Beauty'
Uvularia grandiflora

North-facing aspects
Acanthus spinosus L.
Aconitum 'Spark's Variety'
Ageratina altissima
   'Chocolate'
Ajuga reptans 'Catlin's Giant'
Alchemilla mollis
Alstroemeria 'Orange Glory'
Anaphalis triplinervis
   'Sommerschnee'
Anchusa azurea 'Loddon
   Royalist'
Anemone hupehensis
   'Hadspen Abundance'
A. sylvestris
Angelica sylvestris 'Purpurea'
Aquilegia vulgaris var. stellata
   'Nora Barlow'
Aster × frikartii 'Mönch'
Bergenia 'Bressingham
   White'
Brunnera macrophylla 'Jack
   Frost'

Campanula 'Burghaltii'
C. lactiflora 'Loddon Anna'
Centaurea montana 'Gold
   Bullion'
Cephalaria gigantea
Chaerophyllum hirsutum
   'Roseum'
Chelone glabra
Convallaria majalis
Coreopsis verticillata 'Zagreb'
Cyclamen hederifolium
Darmera peltata
Dicentra spectabilis
Dictamnus albus var.
   purpureus
Digitalis × mertonensis
Doronicum × excelsum
   'Harpur Crewe'
Dracunculus vulgaris
Epimedium grandiflorum
Eranthis hyemalis
Erythronium 'Pagoda'
Euphorbia amygdaloides
   'Purpurea'
E. griffithii 'Dixter'
E. polychroma
Filipendula purpurea
Galanthus nivalis
Gentiana asclepiadea
Geranium 'Jolly Bee'
G. × oxonianum 'Wargrave
   Pink'
G. phaeum
G. psilostemon
Hacquetia epipactis
Helleborus niger
Hepatica nobilis 'Cobalt'
Hosta 'Big Daddy'
H. 'Fire and Ice'
Inula hookeri
Kirengeshoma palmata
Lamium maculatum 'Beacon
   Silver'
Leucanthemum vulgare
Liriope muscari
Lunaria rediviva
Maianthemum racemosum

Myosotidium hortensia
Narcissus 'Doctor Hugh'
N. 'Dutch Master'
Phuopsis stylosa 'Purpurea'
Podophyllum peltatum
Polygonatum odoratum
Primula japonica 'Miller's
   Crimson'
P. vialii
P. vulgaris
Pulmonaria 'Sissinghurst
   White'
Saxifraga 'Cloth of Gold'
Tiarella wherryi
Tricyrtis formosana 'Dark
   Beauty'
Uvularia grandiflora
Veronica umbrosa 'Georgia
   Blue'
Veronicastrum virginicum
   'Album'
Viola odorata 'Wellsiana'

Coastal areas
Achillea 'Summerwine'
Agapanthus 'Blue Giant'
Anemone hupehensis
   'Hadspen Abundance'
A. sylvestris
Astrantia 'Hadspen Blood'
Bergenia 'Bressingham
   White'
Cynara cardunculus
Dianthus 'Becky Robinson'
Doronicum × excelsum
   'Harpur Crewe'
Gaillardia × grandiflora
   'Dazzler'
Inula hookeri
Iris 'Dusky Challenger'
I. 'Sultan's Palace'
I. unguicularis
Kniphofia 'Percy's Pride'
Lythrum salicaria
   'Feuerkerze'
Myosotidium hortensia
Salvia × sylvestris 'Mainacht'

Tanacetum coccineum
'Brenda'
Thermopsis rhombifolia var.
montana
Veronica austriaca subsp.
teucrium 'Royal Blue'

Drought tolerance
Acanthus spinosus L.
Achillea 'Summerwine'
Agapanthus 'Blue Giant'
Agastache 'Blue Fortune'
Ajuga reptans 'Catlin's Giant'
Alchemilla mollis
Allium 'Globemaster'
A. schubertii
A. sphaerocephalon
Anthriscus sylvestris
'Ravenswing'
Aquilegia vulgaris var. *stellata*
'Nora Barlow'
Asphodelus albus
Aster × *frikartii* 'Mönch'
Bergenia 'Bressingham
White'
Brunnera macrophylla 'Jack
Frost'
Canna 'Wyoming'
Centaurea montana 'Gold
Bullion'
Chaenorhinum origanifolium
'Blue Dream'
Commelina tuberosa
Coelestis Group
Coreopsis verticillata 'Zagreb'
Crambe cordifolia
Crinum × *powellii*
Cynara cardunculus
Dianthus 'Becky Robinson'
Dictamnus albus var.
purpureus
Digitalis × *mertonensis*
Dracunculus vulgaris
Echinacea purpurea 'Robert
Bloom'
Echinops ritro 'Veitch's Blue'
Erigeron karvinskianus
Eryngium bourgatii Graham
Stuart Thomas
Euphorbia amygdaloides
'Purpurea'
E. polychroma
Gaillardia × *grandiflora*
'Dazzler'
Gaura lindheimeri
Geranium (Cinereum
Group) 'Ballerina'
G. 'Jolly Bee'

G. phaeum
Gypsophila 'Rosenschleier'
Helenium 'Sahin's Early
Flowerer'
Helleborus niger
Hemerocallis 'Whichford'
Hesperis matronalis
Incarvillea delavayi
Iris unguicularis
Knautia macedonica
Kniphofia 'Percy's Pride'
Lamium maculatum 'Beacon
Silver'
Lathyrus vernus
Leucanthemum vulgare
Liriope muscari
Lunaria rediviva
Lychnis × *arkwrightii*
'Vesuvius'
Nepeta × *faassenii*
Nerine bowdenii
Oenothera fruticosa
'Fyrverkeri'
Papaver nudicaule
Gartenzwerg Group
P. orientale 'Patty's Plum'
Phlomis russeliana
Phuopsis stylosa 'Purpurea'
Sedum spathulifolium 'Cape
Blanco'
S. telephium Atropurpureum
Group
Sisyrinchium 'E.K. Balls'
Solidago 'Golden Wings'
Stachys byzantina
Thermopsis rhombifolia var.
montana
Tulbaghia violacea 'Alba'
Verbascum (Cotswold
Group) 'Gainsborough'
Verbena bonariensis

Wet, boggy soil
Chelone glabra
Darmera peltata
Filipendula purpurea
Gunnera manicata
Lythrum salicaria 'Feuerkerze'
Rheum palmatum var.
tanguticum
Zantedeschia aethiopica
'Crowborough'

Woodland
Aconitum 'Spark's Variety'
Ajuga reptans 'Catlin's Giant'
Anemone hupehensis
'Hadspen Abundance'

Aquilegia vulgaris var. *stellata*
'Nora Barlow'
Asphodelus albus
Campanula glomerata
'Superba'
Chaerophyllum hirsutum
'Roseum'
Convallaria majalis
Coreopsis verticillata 'Zagreb'
Corydalis 'Kingfisher'
Cyclamen hederifolium
Darmera peltata
Dicentra spectabilis
Digitalis × *mertonensis*
Eranthis hyemalis
Erythronium 'Pagoda'
Euphorbia amygdaloides
'Purpurea'
E. griffithii 'Dixter'
Filipendula purpurea
Gentiana asclepiadea
Geranium phaeum
Gillenia trifoliata
Gunnera manicata
Hacquetia epipactis
Hepatica nobilis 'Cobalt'
Hesperis matronalis
Hosta 'Big Daddy'
Inula hookeri
Kirengeshoma palmata
Lamium maculatum 'Beacon
Silver'
Liriope muscari
Lunaria rediviva
Lychnis × *arkwrightii*
'Vesuvius'
Maianthemum racemosum
Meconopsis betonicifolia
Narcissus 'Doctor Hugh'
Omphalodes cappadocica
'Cherry Ingram'
Persicaria affinis 'Darjeeling
Red'
Podophyllum peltatum
Polemonium 'Lambrook
Mauve'
Polygonatum odoratum
Primula vulgaris
Pulmonaria 'Sissinghurst
White'
Ranunculus aconitifolius 'Flore
Pleno'
Tellima grandiflora
Thalictrum aquilegiifolium
'Thundercloud'
Thermopsis rhombifolia var.
montana
Tiarella wherryi

Tricyrtis formosana 'Dark
Beauty'
Uvularia grandiflora
Viola odorata 'Wellsiana'

Architectural
Acanthus spinosus L.
Allium schubertii
Astrantia 'Hadspen Blood'
Crambe cordifolia
Cynara cardunculus
Echinops ritro 'Veitch's Blue'
Eryngium bourgatii Graham
Stuart Thomas
Euphorbia amygdaloides
'Purpurea'
Helenium 'Autumn Lollipop'
Kirengeshoma palmata
Rheum palmatum var.
tanguticum
Sisyrinchium 'E.K. Balls'

Containers
Agapanthus 'Blue Giant'
Alstroemeria 'Orange Glory'
Aster × *frikartii* 'Mönch'
Canna 'Wyoming'
Commelina tuberosa
Coelestis Group
Corydalis 'Kingfisher'
Crinum × *powellii*
Dianthus 'Becky Robinson'
Doronicum × *excelsum*
'Harpur Crewe'
Erigeron karvinskianus
Euphorbia polychroma
Galanthus nivalis
Geranium 'Jolly Bee'
Geum 'Prinses Juliana'
Hemerocallis 'Whichford'
Hesperis matronalis
Heuchera 'Persian Carpet'
Hosta 'Big Daddy'
H. 'Fire and Ice'
Leucanthemum vulgare
Lilium 'Miss Lucy'
Liriope muscari
Narcissus 'Doctor Hugh'
Nerine bowdenii
Oenothera fruticosa
'Fyrverkeri'
Phuopsis stylosa '
Purpurea'
Platycodon grandiflorus
Potentilla atrosanguinea
Primula japonica 'Miller's
Crimson'
P. vulgaris

Pulsatilla vulgaris 'Röde
  Klokke'
Schizostylis coccinea 'Jennifer'
Silene schafta
Tulipa 'Green Wave'
T. 'Queen of Night'
Uvularia grandiflora
Veronica umbrosa 'Georgia
  Blue'
Viola sororia 'Freckles'

Ground cover
Ajuga reptans 'Catlin's Giant'
Alchemilla mollis
Aquilegia vulgaris var. stellata
  'Nora Barlow'
Bergenia 'Bressingham
  White'
Brunnera macrophylla 'Jack
  Frost'
Convallaria majalis
Cyclamen hederifolium
Dracunculus vulgaris
Epimedium grandiflorum
Eranthis hyemalis
Filipendula purpurea
Geranium (Cinereum
  Group) 'Ballerina'
G. 'Jolly Bee'
G. × oxonianum 'Wargrave
  Pink'
G. phaeum
G. psilostemon
Hacquetia epipactis
Heuchera 'Persian Carpet'
Hosta 'Big Daddy'
Kirengeshoma palmata
Lamium maculatum 'Beacon
  Silver'
Liriope muscari
Maianthemum racemosum
Myosotidium hortensia
Persicaria affinis 'Darjeeling
  Red'
Phuopsis stylosa
  'Purpurea'
Pulmonaria 'Sissinghurst
  White'
Silene schafta
Stachys byzantina
Tellima grandiflora
Tiarella wherryi
Viola odorata 'Wellsiana'

Red flowers
Achillea 'Summerwine'
Allium sphaerocephalon
Astrantia 'Hadspen Blood'

Chrysanthemum 'Ruby
  Mound'
Dahlia 'Bishop of Llandaff'
Dracunculus vulgaris
Filipendula purpurea
Gunnera manicata
Iris 'Sultan's Palace'
Knautia macedonica
Lobelia cardinalis
Monarda 'Cambridge
  Scarlet'
Papaver orientale 'Patty's
  Plum'
Potentilla atrosanguinea
Primula japonica 'Miller's
  Crimson'
P. vialii
Pulsatilla vulgaris 'Röde
  Klokke'
Rheum palmatum var.
  tanguticum
Sanguisorba 'Tanna'
Tulipa 'Queen of Night'

Pink flowers
Anemone hupehensis
  'Hadspen Abundance'
Angelica sylvestris 'Purpurea'
Aquilegia vulgaris var. stellata
  'Nora Barlow'
Bergenia 'Bressingham
  White'
Campanula lactiflora
  'Loddon Anna'
Chaerophyllum hirsutum
  'Roseum'
Crinum × powellii
Cyclamen hederifolium
Dianthus 'Becky Robinson'
Dicentra spectabilis
Digitalis × mertonensis
Echinacea purpurea 'Robert
  Bloom'
Francoa sonchifolia
Geranium × oxonianum
  'Wargrave Pink'
G. psilostemon
Incarvillea delavayi
Lamium maculatum 'Beacon
  Silver'
Liatris spicata 'Kobold'
Lythrum salicaria 'Feuerkerze'
Macleaya microcarpa
  'Kelway's Coral Plume'
Nerine bowdenii
Persicaria affinis 'Darjeeling
  Red'
Phlox paniculata 'Bright Eyes'

Rodgersia pinnata 'Superba'
Schizostylis coccinea 'Jennifer'
Sedum telephium
  Atropurpureum Group
Silene schafta
Tanacetum coccineum
  'Brenda'
Tiarella wherryi
Tulipa 'Green Wave'

Lilac/purple/lavender
flowers
Aconitum 'Spark's Variety'
Allium 'Globemaster'
A. schubertii
Aster × frikartii 'Mönch'
Campanula 'Burghaltii'
C. glomerata 'Superba'
Chaenorhinum origanifolium
  'Blue Dream'
Cynara cardunculus
Dictamnus albus var.
  purpureus
Dracunculus vulgaris
Geranium (Cinereum
  Group) 'Ballerina'
G. 'Jolly Bee'
G. phaeum
Hesperis matronalis
Hosta 'Fire and Ice'
Iris 'Dusky Challenger'
I. unguicularis
Lathyrus vernus
Lunaria rediviva
Lupinus 'The Governor'
Penstemon 'Blackbird'
Phuopsis stylosa 'Purpurea'
Polemonium 'Lambrook
  Mauve'
Stachys byzantina
Thalictrum aquilegiifolium
  'Thundercloud'
Tricyrtis formosana 'Dark
  Beauty'
Verbena bonariensis
Viola odorata 'Wellsiana'
V. sororia 'Freckles'

Blue flowers
Agapanthus 'Blue Giant'
Agastache 'Blue Fortune'
Ajuga reptans 'Catlin's Giant'
Anchusa azurea 'Loddon
  Royalist'
Brunnera macrophylla 'Jack
  Frost'
Centaurea montana 'Gold
  Bullion'

Commelina tuberosa
  Coelestis Group
Corydalis 'Kingfisher'
Delphinium 'Blue Nile'
Echinops ritro 'Veitch's Blue'
Eryngium bourgatii Graham
  Stuart Thomas
Gentiana asclepiadea
Hepatica nobilis 'Cobalt'
Liriope muscari
Meconopsis betonicifolia
Myosotidium hortensia
Nepeta × faassenii
Omphalodes cappadocica
  'Cherry Ingram'
Platycodon grandiflorus
Salvia × sylvestris 'Mainacht'
Sisyrinchium 'E.K. Balls'
Tradescantia Andersoniana
  Group 'Zwanenburg Blue'
Veronica austriaca subsp.
  teucrium 'Royal Blue'
V. umbrosa 'Georgia Blue'

Orange flowers
Alstroemeria 'Orange Glory'
Canna 'Wyoming'
Euphorbia griffithii 'Dixter'
Gaillardia × grandiflora
  'Dazzler'
Geum 'Prinses Juliana'
Helenium 'Sahin's Early
  Flowerer'
Lychnis × arkwrightii
  'Vesuvius'
Papaver nudicaule
  Gartenzwerg Group

Yellow flowers
Alchemilla mollis
Cephalaria gigantea
Coreopsis verticillata 'Zagreb'
Doronicum × excelsum
  'Harpur Crewe'
Eranthis hyemalis
Erythronium 'Pagoda'
Euphorbia amygdaloides
  'Purpurea'
E. polychroma
Helenium 'Autumn Lollipop'
Hemerocallis 'Whichford'
Inula hookeri
Kirengeshoma palmata
Narcissus 'Dutch Master'
Oenothera fruticosa
  'Fyrverkeri'
Phlomis russeliana
Primula vulgaris

Rudbeckia fulgida var.
 sullivantii 'Goldsturm'
Saxifraga 'Cloth of Gold'
Sedum spathulifolium 'Cape
 Blanco'
Solidago 'Golden Wings'
S. × luteus 'Lemore'
Thermopsis rhombifolia var.
 montana
Trollius × cultorum 'Alabaster'
Uvularia grandiflora
Verbascum (Cotswold
 Group) 'Gainsborough'

Green flowers
Gunnera manicata
Hacquetia epipactis
Kniphofia 'Percy's Pride'
Tellima grandiflora
Tulipa 'Green Wave'

Cream/white flowers
Acanthus spinosus L.
Ageratina altissima
 'Chocolate'
Anaphalis triplinervis
 'Sommerschnee'
Anemone sylvestris
Anthericum liliago 'Major'
Anthriscus sylvestris
 'Ravenswing'
Asphodelus albus
Bergenia 'Bressingham
 White'
Chelone glabra
Convallaria majalis
Crambe cordifolia
Darmera peltata
Epimedium grandiflorum
Erigeron karvinskianus
Galanthus nivalis

Gaura lindheimeri
Gillenia trifoliata
Gypsophila 'Rosenschleier'
Helleborus niger
Heuchera 'Persian
 Carpet'
Hosta 'Big Daddy'
Leucanthemum vulgare
Lilium 'Miss Lucy'
Maianthemum racemosum
Narcissus 'Doctor Hugh'
Paeonia 'Claire de Lune'
P. lactiflora 'Duchesse de
 Nemours'
Physostegia virginiana
 'Summer Snow'
Podophyllum peltatum
Polygonatum odoratum
Pulmonaria 'Sissinghurst
 White'

Ranunculus aconitifolius 'Flore
 Pleno'
Saxifraga 'Cloth of Gold'
Tellima grandiflora
Tiarella wherryi
Trollius × cultorum 'Alabaster'
Tulbaghia violacea 'Alba'
Veronicastrum virginicum
 'Album'
Viola sororia 'Freckles'
Zantedeschia aethiopica
 'Crowborough'

Plant index

Acanthus spinosus L. 35
Achillea 'Summerwine' 54
Aconitum 'Spark's Variety' 70
Agapanthus 'Blue Giant' 70
Agastache 'Blue Fortune' 83
Ageratina altissima
 'Chocolate' 71
Ajuga reptans 'Catlin's Giant'
 10
Alchemilla mollis 36
Allium 'Globemaster' 37
A. schubertii 11
A. sphaerocephalon 37
Alstroemeria 'Orange Glory'
 54
Anaphalis triplinervis
 'Sommerschnee' 90
Anchusa azurea 'Loddon
 Royalist' 55
Anemone hupehensis
 'Hadspen Abundance' 95
A. sylvestris 11
Angelica sylvestris 'Purpurea'
 71
Anthericum liliago 'Major' 29
Anthriscus sylvestris
 'Ravenswing' 29

Aquilegia vulgaris var. stellata
 'Nora Barlow' (Barlow
 Series) 30
Asphodelus albus 30
Aster × frikartii 'Mönch' 90
Astrantia 'Hadspen Blood'
 38

Bergenia 'Bressingham
 White' 12
Brunnera macrophylla
 'Jack Frost' 12

Campanula 'Burghaltii' 39
C. glomerata 'Superba' 39
C. lactiflora 'Loddon Anna'
 72
Canna 'Wyoming' 72
Centaurea montana 'Gold
 Bullion' 13
Cephalaria gigantea 73
Chaenorhinum origanifolium
 'Blue Dream' 40
Chaerophyllum hirsutum
 'Roseum' 13
Chelone glabra 55
Chrysanthemum 'Ruby
 Mound' 84

Commelina tuberosa
 Coelestis Group 84
Convallaria majalis 14
Coreopsis verticillata 'Zagreb'
 40
Corydalis 'Kingfisher' 14
Crambe cordifolia 73
Crinum × powellii 74
Cyclamen hederifolium 85
Cynara cardunculus 74

Dahlia 'Bishop of Llandaff'
 91
Darmera peltata 35
Delphinium 'Blue Nile'
 75
Dianthus 'Becky Robinson'
 41
Dicentra spectabilis 31
Dictamnus albus var.
 purpureus 56
Digitalis × mertonensis 56
Doronicum × excelsum
 'Harpur Crewe' 31
Dracunculus vulgaris 75

Echinacea purpurea 'Robert
 Bloom' 57

Echinops ritro 'Veitch's Blue'
 57
Epimedium grandiflorum 15
Eranthis hyemalis 98
Erigeron karvinskianus 85
Eryngium bourgatii Graham
 Stuart Thomas 41
Erythronium 'Pagoda' 15
Euphorbia amygdaloides
 'Purpurea' 16
E. griffithii 'Dixter' 58
E. polychroma 17

Filipendula purpurea 76
Francoa sonchifolia 58

Gaillardia × grandiflora
 'Dazzler' 91
Galanthus nivalis 99
Gaura lindheimeri 96
Gentiana asclepiadea 59
Geranium (Cinereum
 Group) 'Ballerina' 42
G. 'Jolly Bee' 43
G. × oxonianum 'Wargrave
 Pink' 86
G. phaeum 59
G. psilostemon 76

Geum 'Prinses Juliana' 43
Gillenia trifoliata 60
Gunnera manicata 77
Gypsophila 'Rosenschleier'
    (syn. G. 'Rosy Veil') 44

Hacquetia epipactis 17
Helenium 'Autumn Lollipop'
    92
H. 'Sahin's Early Flowerer'
    60
Helleborus niger 99
Hemerocallis 'Whichford' 61
Hepatica nobilis 'Cobalt' 18
Hesperis matronalis 61
Heuchera 'Persian Carpet'
    44
Hosta 'Big Daddy'
    (sieboldiana hybrid) 18
H. 'Fire and Ice' 45

Incarvillea delavayi 45
Inula hookeri 92
Iris 'Dusky Challenger' (TB)
    77
I. 'Sultan's Palace' (TB) 62
I. unguicularis 100

Kirengeshoma palmata 78
Knautia macedonica 62
Kniphofia 'Percy's Pride' 96

Lamium maculatum 'Beacon
    Silver' 46
Lathyrus vernus 19
Leucanthemum vulgare 63
Liatris spicata 'Kobold' 46
Lilium 'Miss Lucy' 78
Liriope muscari 86
Lobelia cardinalis 93
Lunaria rediviva 63

Lupinus 'The Governor'
    (Band of Nobles Series)
    64
Lychnis × arkwrightii
    'Vesuvius' 79
Lythrum salicaria
    'Feuerkerze' (syn. L.s.
    Firecandle) 79

Macleaya microcarpa
    'Kelway's Coral Plume' 80
Maianthemum racemosum
    32
Meconopsis betonicifolia 80
Monarda 'Cambridge
    Scarlet' 64
Myosotidium hortensia 19

Narcissus 'Doctor Hugh' 20
N. 'Dutch Master' 20
Nepeta × faassenii 47
Nerine bowdenii 87

Oenothera fruticosa
    'Fyrverkeri' (syn.
    O.f. Fireworks) 47
Omphalodes cappadocica
    'Cherry Ingram' 21

Paeonia 'Claire de Lune' 32
P. lactiflora 'Duchesse
    de Nemours' 65
Papaver nudicaule
    Gartenzwerg Group 48
P. orientale 'Patty's Plum' 66
Penstemon 'Blackbird' 93
Persicaria affinis 'Darjeeling
    Red' 48
Phlomis russeliana 66
Phlox paniculata 'Bright Eyes'
    94

Phuopsis stylosa 'Purpurea'
    49
Physostegia virginiana
    'Summer Snow' 87
Platycodon grandiflorus 49
Podophyllum peltatum 21
Polemonium 'Lambrook
    Mauve' 50
Polygonatum odoratum 33
Potentilla atrosanguinea 67
Primula japonica 'Miller's
    Crimson' 22
P. vialli 50
P. vulgaris 23
Pulmonaria 'Sissinghurst
    White' 23
Pulsatilla vulgaris 'Röde
    Klokke' 24

Ranunculus aconitifolius
    'Flore Pleno' 24
Rheum palmatum var.
    tanguticum 81
Rodgersia pinnata 'Superba'
    81
Rudbeckia fulgida var.
    sullivantii 'Goldsturm' 94

Salvia × sylvestris 'Mainacht'
    67
Sanguisorba 'Tanna' 51
Saxifraga 'Cloth of Gold'
    (exarta subsp. moschata)
    25
Schizostylis coccinea 'Jennifer'
    88
Sedum spathulifolium 'Cape
    Blanco' 51
S. telephium Atropurpureum
    Group 88

Silene schafta 89
Sisyrinchium 'E.K. Balls' 25
Solidago 'Golden Wings' 97
S. × luteus 'Lemore' 68
Stachys byzantina 52

Tanacetum coccineum
    'Brenda' 68
Tellima grandiflora 33
Thalictrum aquilegiifolium
    'Thundercloud' 69
Thermopsis rhombifolia var.
    montana 69
Tiarella wherryi 26
Tradescantia Andersoniana
    Group 'Zwanenburg
    Blue' 89
Tricyrtis formosana 'Dark
    Beauty' 52
Trollius × cultorum 'Alabaster'
    26
Tulbaghia violacea 'Alba' 53
Tulipa 'Green Wave' 27
T. 'Queen of Night' 27

Uvularia grandiflora 34

Verbascum (Cotswold
    Group) 'Gainsborough'
    82
Verbena bonariensis 97
Veronica austriaca subsp.
    teucrium 'Royal Blue' 53
V. umbrosa 'Georgia Blue' 28
Veronicastrum virginicum
    'Album' 82
Viola odorata 'Wellsiana' 100
V. sororia 'Freckles' 28

Zantedeschia aethiopica
    'Crowborough' 34

Picture credits

All photographs supplied by Garden World Images

Lilium 'Miss Lucy' (p.78) © Jonathan Buckley; Tulbaghia violacea 'Alba' (p.53) © bulbargence.com; Centaurea montana 'Gold Bullion' (p.13), Tulipa 'Green Wave' (p.27), Geum 'Prinses Juliana' (p.43), Heuchera 'Persian Carpet' (p.44), Papaver nudicaule Gartenzwerg Group (p.48), Veronica austriaca subsp. teucrium 'Royal Blue' (p.53), Iris 'Sultan's Palace' (p.62), Cephalaria gigantea (p.73), Lychnis × arkwrightii 'Vesuvius' (p.79), Macleaya microcarpa 'Kelway's Coral Plume' (p.80), Silene schafta (p.89) © Floramedia; Pulsatilla vulgaris 'Röde Klokke' (p.24) © PPWW/Daan Smit; Hepatica nobilis 'Cobalt' (p.18) © Slack Top nurseries; Helenium 'Autumn Lollipop' (p.92) © Thompson & Morgan